75 years of
Maynes
buses and coaches

by

Mark Hughes MCIT

Venture *publications*

© August 1995 - Mark Hughes

ISBN 1 898432 70 8 card covered

ISBN 1 898432 71 6 casebound

Front Cover Illustration

To celebrate the 75th Anniversary Mayne's painted one of the 1995 delivery of Scania double-deckers in the former company livery of maroon and turquoise, bringing back memories of an earlier age. Number 11 is seen in Piccadilly on a bright sunny morning in July 1995, en route to the Arndale Bus Station.

[Photo: John A. Senior

Produced for the Publishers
Venture Publications, Glossop Derbyshire,
by Mopok Graphics, Glossop SK13 8EH
using computerised origination

CONTENTS

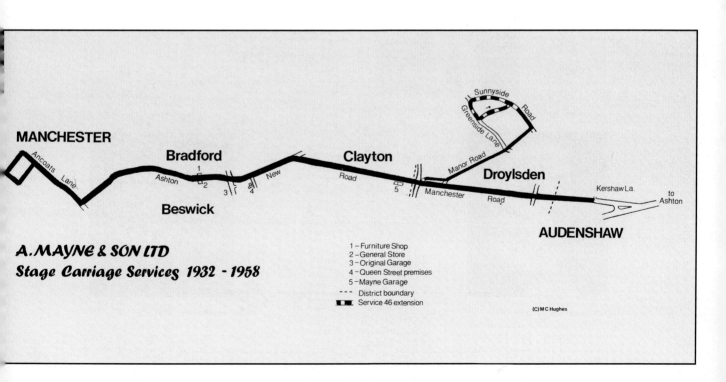

MANCHESTER

Bradford

Clayton

Sunnyside

Droylsden

Beswick

AUDENSHAW

to Ashton

A. MAYNE & SON LTD
Stage Carriage Services 1932 - 1958

1 – Furniture Shop
2 – General Store
3 – Original Garage
4 – Queen Street premises
5 – Mayne Garage
- - - District boundary
▮▮▮ Service 46 extension

(C) M C Hughes

FOREWORD

I would like to thank Mark Hughes for writing this book which I have seen grow and develop over the last year. It is perhaps because I have been involved with our family business for as long as I can remember that, when the idea of such a work was first put to me, I found it difficult to understand why other people should be concerned about the history and development of a small coach and bus company. Having now read the completed book, I am convinced the story it has to tell will prove interesting to the wider public as well as bus and coach enthusiasts.

This year we celebrate the Company's 75th anniversary and also the 100th anniversary of my father's birth. My father was in his 'fifties when I was born and he would often tell stories of the early days of the business. Perhaps we should be claiming a longer period than 75 years, since we became involved with transport well before the First World War. I remember in particular one of my father's stories which concerned the horse and cart used by my grandfather to deliver furniture. Evidently, when the time came for the horse to be put to grass, it became so excited on this, the first occasion it had been in an open field, that it tried to jump the field gate; it broke its leg and had to be destroyed. The Company has proved to be more successful with machines than animals.

The greatest value for me of this book is that it has made me recall the host of people whose hard work and dedication have been responsible for the development of the Company over the years. There have been so many of them that it would be wrong to attempt to single out any individuals, whether management, mechanics or drivers. I would like to thank them all. I particularly hope that those who are still able to read this book will enjoy it as much as I have.

Stephen B. Mayne
Chairman and Managing Director,
A. Mayne & Son Ltd.

September 1995

Arthur Mayne Snr (1873-1935)
As a boy he roamed the streets of Salford selling newspapers, and later became the founder of three successful family businesses.

Arthur Mayne Jnr (1895-1980)
Guided the company's fortunes for sixty years, steadily developing it into the area's principal independent bus and coach operator.

INTRODUCTION

My very first journey on a Maynes bus occurred in the Summer of 1983 when I travelled on a Bristol VR to visit a prospective high school in Littlemoss. Although the school's facilities were more than satisfactory, it was the bus journey back which proved to be the deciding factor.

In those days we lived in Droylsden and each morning I would wait with my friends at the bus stop opposite Mayne Garage and watch the activity within until the bus arrived to take us to school. The simple fact that these buses were so much different than the other Manchester buses made me curious, and I began to learn what little I could about the company and its vehicles.

My friends, having long since agreed that the country air had gone to my head, were quick to test that knowledge and many was the time when they were completely baffled by my ability to correctly identify an approaching Maynes vehicle. Their good-natured banter would also prompt me to learn the timetable to such an extent that I could often tell them, long before we had even left the classroom, which bus would be taking us home.

When it came to deciding on a career therefore, the choice seemed obvious and a job in the office at Maynes would probably have suited me down to the ground. Unfortunately my letter enquiring if there were any vacancies went unanswered and so, in July 1988, I went to work for Shearings in Wigan. A move to Greater Manchester PTE in 1989 would bring me into closer contact with the management at Maynes but, like many other enthusiasts before me, I found the door to so many answers continued to remain firmly closed.

All that changed in 1990 when one of my bosses at the PTE moved to Maynes and I would like to record my appreciation of that introduction from Martin Knisz. I would also like express my heartfelt gratitude to everyone at Maynes who has given me so much encouragement and assistance over these last few years. In particular I would like to thank Gradyn Thompson, the company's general manager, for finding the answers to so many questions and for enduring my seemingly endless stream of telephone calls.

The files and records of both the Omnibus Society and PSV Circle have also been an invaluable aid. Individual members of those organisations have also been most generous with their assistance and particular mention should be made of Graham Ashworth for his help in putting together the fleet history and to Peter Deegan for his initial research.

I also record my thanks to Tommy Proctor, a retired garage foreman, whose fifty years service with Maynes helped bring some of those early years to life and to Eric Ogden and Jon Brierley who read the proofs and made many helpful suggestions.

A very special thank you must also go to my fellow Maynes enthusiast, Brian Lomas, who so generously made available his extensive photographic collection and without whose help this book would have contained few pictures.

Finally I would like to thank Stephen Mayne for writing the Foreword and Mrs Olive Mayne for providing the information on her late husband, Arthur Mayne – the man who made this story worth telling and to whom I would like to dedicate this book.

Mark Hughes
Audenshaw
September 1995

Chapter One
Arthur Mayne – Pioneer

Mayne is a name that has long been associated with the running of buses and coaches in the Manchester area. Indeed it is one of the City's oldest-established road transport businesses which has managed to survive, relatively unchanged, throughout several eventful decades, outlasting even the largest of its competitors.

For many years the Mayne family ran a general store and a furniture shop in the Bradford district of the City. Arthur Mayne, an upholsterer by trade, opened the furniture store in the late 19th century on a turnpike road which ran between Manchester and the industrial town of Ashton-under-Lyne. The shop was located next to the Moseley Hotel on Ashton New Road and Arthur and his wife Matilda lived in the rooms above.

The first of their five children was born in 1895 and through the continuing hard work of their father, the family eventually acquired another shop across the road. This was re-opened as a general store and became the domain of Matilda Mayne who was assisted by her four daughters Matilda, Alice, Olive and Lena. Her eldest child, Arthur Junior, wanted to follow in the footsteps of his father and after leaving school in 1909 began an apprenticeship in the family's furniture business, which became known as A. Mayne & Son.

Nine years later, the assassination of an Archduke in a dusty town called Sarajevo would plunge Europe into chaos and forever alter the life of young Arthur. When Britain declared war on Germany in August 1914, the teenager immediately joined up, becoming a Medical Orderly with the Royal Army Medical Corps. Whilst he may not have been directly involved in the fighting, his role still carried an immense amount of danger and he subsequently returned home suffering from pneumonia and the effects of a gas attack. Eventually nursed back to health, it was soon realised that Arthur's career in the upholstery business was now at an end, as the toxins used in the profession would only aggravate his disability.

Prior to the Great War, the family had delivered their furniture products with the help of a horse and cart and, as an outside job was called for, it was decided that the twenty-five year old should enter the motor transport industry. The first vehicle purchased by the family concern was a Ford Model-T van which was acquired in 1920 and Arthur put this to immediate use delivering furniture and small consignments of goods on behalf of the family stores.

During his service with the RAMC, Arthur would have become familiar with a Walthamstow-based manufacturer known as AEC. The Associated Equipment Company had supplied around 8,000 of its rugged 3-ton lorries to the War Department, a large number of which were later converted for civilian use. In 1923, Arthur Junior purchased one of these lorries, which were known as the Y-type, and placed it in service alongside the Ford which he garaged near Howarth Street (now Howarth Close) on Grey Mare Lane, Beswick. Arthur had joined a local co-operative by this time which traded under the name of 'Pioneer' and the ruggedness of the former military vehicle soon became an excellent asset.

In the fashion of that period, the goods body on the Y-type could be demounted from the chassis and a charabanc body dropped in its place. This enabled Arthur to run excursions for the local populace at the weekend. Early destinations included the coastal resorts of

An early pioneer charabanc, carrying bodywork of a type applied to variety of chassis in the early days, this one being notable for the use of pneumatic tyres on disc wheels on the front axle and solid tyres on spoked wheels at the rear. This would relate to the heavier loading on the rear axle, evidently in excess of the capacity of the pneumatics on the front axle.

Blackpool, Southport and Morecambe, the spa town of Buxton and the lakes at Pickmere and Hollingworth.

While the operation of the haulage business was considered a year round task the development of suburban motor coaching was found to be particularly seasonal in character. The surrounding towns had expanded tremendously due to the tide of industrial growth in the area. Against a background of the fields and farms of Droylsden and Audenshaw were the industrial suburbs of Beswick, Clayton, Openshaw and Gorton. Many of those who lived in the area would have worked in the engineering, chemical and cotton industries which operated a five-and-a-half day week and thereby limited any profitable excursions to Sundays, the major holiday weekends (Easter, Whitsuntide and August) and the annual Wakes holidays.

Despite these limited opportunities, Arthur Junior steered the new venture into a period of prosperity. Under the watchful eye and guiding hand of his father, the growing expertise of young Arthur would bring increased work to the passenger section, introducing trips to football matches and race meetings. This growth of the coaching business was timely, for the development of the vehicles used by the industry would soon see the introduction of coach-built bodies that were more substantial in their construction.

The Mayne family considered the potential of the coaching 'section' to be worthy of continuation, and the arrival of the first purpose-built coaches in 1925 was followed within a short period by the decision to close the haulage operations down, leaving Arthur Junior free to concentrate on the carriage of his human 'cargo'.

Motor charabanc and coach operators were regulated under the provisions of the Town Police Clauses Act of 1847, as the selling of seats by the kerb-side was regarded as plying for hire under the Hackney Carriage provisions of the act, which had originally been passed to regulate the operation of hansom cabs in city centres. The City of Manchester operated an 'open house' policy for motor charabancs, provided the owners were local ratepayers, and so Arthur Mayne had little problem in securing licences to operate excursions beyond the city boundaries.

Maynes first purpose built vehicles consisted of an AEC 416 and a more powerful AEC 509. The 416 model was AEC's best selling motor coach of the 1920s whilst the 509 had its origins in the early Y-type lorry. This increase in vehicles no doubt required a change of premises and Arthur sold his land on Grey Mare Lane to a man who later developed the site into a petrol filling station. Arthur's new premises, located next to the local school on Queen Street (now Quinn Street) offered room for expansion and was a short distance away from the main Ashton New Road in Beswick.

Arthur Mayne now inaugurated the first regular coach service from the towns of Ashton-under-Lyne, Audenshaw, Droylsden, Clayton and Beswick direct to Blackpool. Although the 55 mile journey initially took more than 3½ hours to complete, the service was an immediate success. Maynes Premier Motors, as his firm had become known, continued to run excursions from the Bradford and Beswick areas of the city, as well as transporting passengers from other neighbouring towns to their Wakes Week destinations.

The Droylsden Omnibus Services

Although the licensing policy of Manchester Corporation was quite liberal towards motor coach operators, the City was extremely reluctant to licence the operation of omnibuses to any operator other than its own Transport Department. The City's policy was influenced by its large investment in its electric tramways and the Watch Committee used powers under the Town Police Clauses Act to eliminate possible competition with its tramway (a situation that was

intended by the original provisions of the Act).

Even though the Manchester Corporation Tramways Department had run some omnibuses, generally on routes that were complementary to the tramways, the vast majority of journeys within the city's boundaries were taken by tramcar. The tram routes also operated through the town centres of neighbouring authorities, with joint operations bringing other municipal tramcars into Manchester's central areas. There was therefore a great deal of co-operation between the various authorities in the area, and policy regarding potentially-competitive omnibus routes was generally uniform.

The depression and social unrest that followed the Great War continued into the 1920s, and the Coal Strikes of 1921 brought many of the tramway services to a halt as supplies to power stations dwindled. At this time authorities issued temporary licences to bus and coach firms to provide an alternative service for the public. In 1926, a further spate of public unrest resulted in the General Strike, which crippled the country from 3rd-12th May, and resulted in a number of independent coach operators running temporary services along the tram routes. During the strike, Arthur Mayne and the other members of the Pioneer consortium are understood to have provided such a service along Ashton New Road, in common with other firms who came to the rescue of the otherwise stranded public.

Express Motor Buses

Despite the fact that the tramways were efficiently run, the service provided was often slow, and the development of the motor bus prompted Manchester Tramways Department to look into ways of speeding up journey times for its longer-distance travellers. In February 1927, it established the principle of express omnibus routes that would parallel the tram routes along the main arteries, but would run across the city centre. Fares would be set at double the rates of the tramways with a 2d minimum fare along tram routes and a fare of 1d elsewhere. This would restrict local traffic but make longer journeys attractive in view of the shortened running times. The co-operation already evident between the tramway owning authorities soon led to the scheme being extended to provide fast interurban services, a conference of nine neighbouring authorities agreeing in August 1927 to participate in the new venture.

Meanwhile, the first of six initial routes was coming into operation, although progress on the route intended to serve the Ashton New Road corridor (Droylsden-Manchester-Old Trafford-Stretford-Urmston) was delayed as a result of the refusal of Stretford Urban District Council to issue the necessary licences. Stretford UDC owned its own tramway system, and had leased it to Manchester, receiving revenue for allowing the trams to run through the town en-route to Sale and Altrincham. This income was then used to reduce the loans set up to finance its construction. Stretford was not willing to licence omnibuses that would dilute the tramway traffic unless it could participate in the revenue of the proposed omnibuses as well. As a result, Manchester had to introduce a truncated service between Droylsden and Manchester (Stevenson Square) on 18th October 1927, the start of which was followed one month later by a rival operation.

The Pioneer Begins

James Albert Ferrington, trading as the 'Pioneer Motor Bus Service', had been a member of the Pioneer haulage consortium, and retained use of the title for his new omnibus venture which operated between Droylsden and Manchester (Hilton Street Garage). Ferrington was licensed in Droylsden and initially ran express through Clayton and Beswick. By charging fares that were a lot closer to the tram fares than

Here a party of what were rather tactlessly described as fatherless children are ready to set off on an excursion trip in three vehicles led by a Dennis, NA 9763, evidently a 4-ton model as built for military use in the 1914-18 war and continued in production for several years thereafter. The charabanc body had been transferred from a shorter chassis, perhaps hastily since no attempt had been made to disguise the redundant wheel arch, while the front of the old body had been married to front doors which may have come from another source with some pieces of board to fill the gap.

the Manchester express buses his service soon grew in popularity.

To counter the threat, Manchester continued to add to and amend its services after concluding operating agreements with Ashton-under-Lyne Corporation and the Stalybridge, Hyde, Mossley & Dukinfield Joint Board. Even Salford Corporation's buses briefly operated along Ashton New Road running between Weaste, Manchester, Ashton and Stalybridge.

After a complete reorganisation on 30th January 1928, the existing services were diverted away from Ashton New Road. To replace them, a new service was introduced between Ashton, Droylsden, Manchester, Chorlton and Urmston in a joint venture with Ashton Corporation. This revised route no longer paralleled Stretford's tramway route, and was able to utilise licences already issued in connection with the Chorlton to Barton omnibus route (the ancestor of today's 22 route).

The situation was further complicated from 1st March 1928, when the privately-owned North Western Road Car Company was admitted to the list of Manchester's approved operators, and several new routes were planned with that company as sole or joint operator. Among these was a route from Glossop and Stalybridge which was extended via Ashton, Audenshaw, Droylsden and Clayton to Manchester (Lwr Mosley St), operating jointly with Manchester and Ashton Corporations and the SHMD Joint Board.

Ferrington, meanwhile, was continuing to run his 'Pioneer' service between Droylsden and Manchester, but sought (in June 1928) to extend the service across the city centre to Stretford. This would have placed him on an even footing with the municipal operators and their associates, but Stretford (still negotiating for financial involvement in any municipal operation along the Chester

Road tramway) was in no mood to sanction independent operation and gave Ferrington short shrift. A repeat application six months later would receive a similarly-worded reply.

Manchester was by this time growing concerned at the inability of its new omnibus services to dispose of the operations of Ferrington (and other independent omnibus operators who were running into the city), and decided to take further steps to eliminate the competition. At this period the Manchester City Police was effectively under the control of the Watch Committee, which instructed the Chief Constable to detail men to concentrate on unearthing any violations of regulations made by the independent omnibus operators. These investigations took place over a six week period commencing in the last week of September 1928 and resulted in a spate of prosecutions in the closing months of the year.

The penalties imposed on Ferrington's 'Pioneer' coupled with his inability to extend the service across Manchester appear to have caused him to reconsider his position as a licenced omnibus operator. Early in 1929 he approached Arthur Mayne with a view to selling him the route, including his small, but modern fleet of Crossley and Dennis single-deckers. Both Arthur Mayne and James Ferrington now applied to Manchester City Council for licences to operate in the city. Ferrington applied for the first time merely to secure a licence confirming his existing operation and upon issue of such would transfer it to Arthur Mayne. Unsurprisingly, Manchester's Watch Committee rejected both applications on 8th February 1929. Notwithstanding the rejection, Arthur went ahead and purchased the licence for the Droylsden to Manchester route and James Ferrington moved to Blackley to consolidate his share in the North Manchester Motor Owners consortium.

Evidently photographed on the same occasion, this vehicle registered at almost the same time with confusingly similar registration, NA 9673. In this case the body is of the fashionable torpedo type much favoured in the years before and briefly after the 1914-18 war. The chassis appears to be either a Halford or a Belsize.

Another view of the Dennis, with driver leaning on the front wing. Note the brackets for lamps alongside the radiator.

Looking very smart was this Leyland, possibly ex-military chassis, of the style widely known as the RAF type. In this case it was registered in Lancashire as TB 1174. One of the Pioneer's names is seen on the vehicle, G W Leggott and Son, Clayton.

This all-weather Dennis coach is thought to have been acquired from James Ferrington along with a batch of three Crossley Eagles in 1929. VM1279, now running as part of the Maynes Premier Motors operation, is seen outside the firm's Queen Street premises (circa 1930).

The beleaguered trio

Other independent omnibus operators running in East Manchester at the time included Goodfellow Services Ltd and Alphonsus H. Duigenan. Ben Goodfellow had secured a licence to operate from Hyde to Manchester in October 1927, whilst Duigenan – an affiliate of Goodfellow's – had launched a Denton to Manchester service on 8th November 1927. Both operated along Hyde Road and both suffered prosecutions in the police operation during the autumn of 1928.

Goodfellow, Duigenan and now Mayne (along with several others) were effectively operating within the city boundaries illegally. Attempts to gain the necessary licences had resulted in an across-the-board rejection and so a conference of the three beleaguered independent operators was called to decide the next course of action. On 18th March 1929, all three simultaneously notified Manchester's Watch Committee that they intended to appeal to the Minister for Transport against the Corporation's unfair decision.

The Ministry Inquiry ran from 18th-21st July under the chairmanship of the Ministry's Inspector Mr Percy Gray. The case for the independents was that Manchester Corporation's refusal to license the respective services was unreasonable, bearing in mind that many surrounding authorities had already issued licences, and that all services were well supported. In the case of Maynes, service statistics presented at the Inquiry showed that an average of 10,000 passengers per week were now being carried along the company's bus route.

The case of Manchester was presented by Mr. F. Webster, the deputy town clerk, and he alleged that Appeal by Maynes was invalid, as all the evidence presented had been in connection with James Ferrington's operation. Arthur Mayne had not been the operator when the service had commenced and offences committed. Mr A.H.M. Wedderburn, the barrister representing Maynes, conceded that this was so, but pointed out that his client was the successor to the goodwill (and vehicles) of Ferrington's operation. Mr Arthur Docker, appearing for Droylsden Urban District Council, expressed complete satisfaction with Maynes omnibus service, and said that his council would object to the loss of the route and the consequent

monopoly that would ensue. Despite the fact that the Corporation's two competing omnibus services had recently been merged (from 29th May) to operate between Chorlton, Manchester and Glossop, Maynes was still the cheapest provider of an omnibus service along Ashton New Road.

Whilst awaiting the decision of the Minister on the matters presented to his Inspector, Manchester Corporation was again presented with a fresh application by Arthur Mayne to ply in Manchester. He also applied to Audenshaw Parish Council to extend the service to Kershaw Lane and arranged for the purchase of a brand new single-decker bus.

The application to serve Audenshaw was welcomed by its Parish Council and a licence was duly granted. The application to ply in Manchester was not greeted quite so warmly however and the result was not unexpected. Having been summarily refused, Arthur was left with little choice but to carry on regardless and hope that the Minister of Transport would uphold his Appeal.

The minister's decision was announced on the 15th August 1929, but it was not the one the independents wanted to hear, for he had decided to make no order on the Corporation to issue them with licences. In the immediate wake of this Goodfellow, Duigenan and Mayne announced that they were lowering their fares even further and threatened to amalgamate their separate businesses to strengthen their combined effort against the Corporation and its mighty Transport Department.

In the end only Duigenan would succumb to the demands of the municipalities and ceased operating his omnibus service. Goodfellows almost failed to survive, having expanded too rapidly in 1930. The company made an operating agreement with Manchester Corporation in 1931, only to breach it shortly afterwards. A series of prosecutions then followed before Ben Goodfellow sold the business to his competitors in 1933.

Arthur Mayne, no doubt bitterly disappointed with the Minister's decision, was able to continue by the process of passengers from Audenshaw and Droylsden purchasing return tickets, so that they had effectively already paid for their journeys home. This meant he was no longer plying-for-hire within the City of Manchester and the need to use Hilton Street Garage (which was private land and exempt from Corporation jurisdiction) was eliminated. Buses now ran in a loop

from Ancoats Lane (now Great Ancoats Street) down Oldham Street to Piccadilly before heading up Lever Street to collect their return passengers for Droylsden and Audenshaw.

Arthur would continue to come into confrontation with the Corporation, when his coaching operation – Maynes Premier Motors – applied to operate excursions and tours from the City Centre. Manchester's liberal policy on coach operators was by this time causing concern, as the city was felt to be overcrowded with motor coach operators from as far afield as Blackpool, Liverpool and Derbyshire. Arthur, a local ratepayer, was initially refused a licence to work from the City Centre, but a second application in April 1929 was eventually granted from 1st August that year.

The Manchester Watch Committee would further examine Mayne's excursion licences on their renewal in June 1930 and initially recommended refusal – a move that would have left Arthur with just the Pioneer omnibus operation had it succeeded. The

This 1930s line-up shows the assorted fleet of the early Mayne/Pioneer operation. The vehicles are (from left to right) Crossley Eagle, AEC Reliance, Dennis and AEC 509. The Crossley in this view (VM6227) would soon be replaced by a Dennis E-type single-decker and its Warwick body used as the staff canteen.

question of the renewal of Maynes Premier Motors licence was still being considered by the Watch Committee in January 1931, when responsibility passed under the Transport Act 1930 to the Ministry of Transport and its North Western Traffic Commissioner.

Maynes took delivery of their first new bus in the Spring of 1929. AEC's model 660 had been given the type name Reliance and fitted with a newly-developed six-cylinder engine. VR498 was supplied by Harold Rothwell, the AEC distributor for North and East Lancashire, and is believed to have replaced the earlier Y-type charabanc. Unlike the AEC 509 parked behind, the Reliance had a propensity to kangaroo starts, even with a skilled driver behind the wheel.

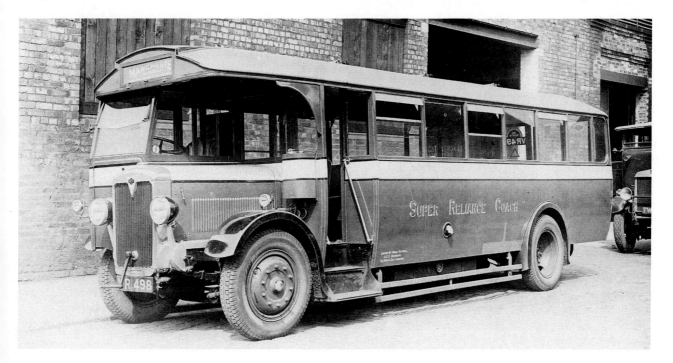

11

Chapter Two
The fight for Road Service Licences

If Arthur Mayne was hoping that he might stand a better chance of obtaining licences under the new system, then he was about to have those hopes quickly dashed. The old licensing system had been replaced by the need for all road passenger operators to hold Road Service Licences, a form of quantity control which would give operators a virtual monopoly on the route they were licensed to provide. The Ministry's Traffic Commissioner, having received an application for such a licence, would publish the details and hold public hearings at which other operators, local authorities and other interested parties could raise objections to the proposals.

Much of Maynes Premier Motors holiday business was for traffic to Blackpool and in accordance with the new legislation and licensing provisions of the Road Traffic Act, Arthur Mayne applied to the Traffic Commissioner to continue operating his excursion and tour programmes from East Manchester – an area which encompassed the districts of Bradford, Beswick, Clayton, Openshaw and Gorton.

Arthur also applied to continue operating his seasonal express service to Blackpool. Under the legislation an express service was a regular-timetabled long distance coach service which charged a minimum fare and ran regardless of the load, whereas an excursion and tour could only operate a limited number of departures in any one season. In the case of the Blackpool service, Maynes could guarantee to fill at least one coach every day and, as it was not unknown to have half the fleet or more employed on this task alone, an express licence with the option of running duplicates was sought.

Objections to the application came from Ashton Corporation,

Ribble, North Western and the London Midland & Scottish Railway, all of which used the services of a professional barrister. The Traffic Commissioner, having been persuaded by the barrister's plea, granted the licence solely in the nature of an excursion and tour with effect from 12th March 1932. Things were already not quite going Arthur's way, when another application (to operate a new express service between Stalybridge and Cleveleys) was turned down following similar objections.

Whilst the company may have already possessed an excursions licence from substantially similar points, the main object of the exercise was to expand the firm's operating base into the town of Stalybridge. To try and achieve this, Arthur applied to extend his existing Blackpool excursion licence, only to be met with increasing opposition at every turn. The extension to Cleveleys was permitted from 8th October 1932 and Arthur would eventually use this as a tool for compromise, offering its surrender in favour of picking up rights in Stalybridge.

After another two lengthy and drawn-out public hearings, the company finally got what it desired, but there was a condition attached however, for the Traffic Commissioner had decided to impose a maximum number of 274 journeys in any one season

VM1279, the former Pioneer Pullman Safety Coach, is seen in the early 1930s having had its front end altered to a half-cab appearance. Its all-weather roof has also been panelled over and the interior fitted with high-back coach seating. The trading name Mayne Coaches is now in use by the firm.

(effective from 1st September 1934). This was a number now identical to, but not in addition to, the maximum number of journeys to Blackpool authorised on the firm's East Manchester licence and would require careful planning on the part of the operator to ensure that this quota was never reached before the end of the season.

Despite this condition, the Blackpool run remained the busiest and most lucrative destination for the company's expanding fleet of motor coaches. Two AEC Regal coaches had been acquired from Hanson of Huddersfield, joining a Leyland Lioness PLC1 acquired in April 1931 from Jos. Bracewell of Blackpool. These were followed in 1933 with the arrival of the firm's first new AEC Regal coach (XJ5574).

The omnibus services 1930

Arthur Mayne lodged an application to continue operating his 'Pioneer' bus service with effect from 24th April 1931. It was hardly surprising to note that objections were placed by Manchester Corporation and also North Western, one of the other providers of the joint omnibus service along Ashton New Road. Also present at the hearing held over the 19th-21st May were representatives from Droylsden UDC and the Clayton Ratepayers. Despite the backing of Droylsden UDC and the thousands of passengers who used Pioneer's service, the application to continue operating was refused.

Arthur Mayne immediately lodged an appeal, which permitted him to continue operating whilst the firm arranged for their case to be better put in the light of the current objections. The Appeal was finally heard some twelve months later on 11th June 1932. Having heard the arguments for and against allowing the independent operator to continue running his omnibus service, the Commissioner chose to grant the licence subject to four conditions.

The first was that the Manchester terminal had to be agreed by both the Commissioner and their biggest rival Manchester Corporation (the use of Piccadilly was obviously deemed far too close for comfort). Secondly, no passengers were to be picked up and set down within the City of Manchester, except by prior agreement with the Corporation. Eventually it was agreed that Maynes could pick up and set down passengers along Ashton New Road, but only those travelling to and from Droylsden and Audenshaw. The company could not carry any passengers travelling solely within the city boundaries. Once across the boundary into Droylsden, however, Maynes could observe all stops from Edge Lane to Audenshaw, as it had been licenced to do under the old system.

All fares were to be determined by the Commissioners (no longer could they charge fares lower than the tram and gain an unfair advantage on their arch rival) and finally, the timetable had to meet the Commissioners' approval and be co-ordinated with the other omnibus services along Ashton New Road.

Under the new licensing system the Traffic Commissioners succeeded in co-ordinating services where the various Watch Committees had largely failed, but it would always be to the advantage of the big operators and municipalities. Most small independent operators who tried to enter the world of stage carriage would find their path blocked by the larger, established operator whose barrister would argue convincingly against permitting such a licence on the grounds that it was unnecessary and would threaten the operations of his client. From now on the running of buses and coaches would be for the smartest and financially fittest. The acquisition race and a new battle for survival had begun.

The other independents

One by one the private bus companies began to disappear. The first to succumb to the pressures of Manchester Corporation was J. R. Tognarelli of Bolton who sold his modern fleet of buses and coaches to his competitors on 9th December 1929. Many other independent omnibus operators of the 1920s would make it into the new licensing system, and all would eventually cross swords with Manchester Corporation and its associates. Goodfellows, Cash of Urmston, H. G. Orr and Sons of Little Lever, Sykes Brothers and Organ and Wachter were all operators who were persuaded to leave the stage carriage arena, one way or another.

Arthur Mayne did not escape unnoticed. The dark blue buses of the 'Pioneer' operation had been operating along the Ashton New Road corridor for eight years, steadily building up a tremendous reputation for a reliable and regular omnibus service. The route continued to flourish, despite keen competition from the municipalities and the mighty North Western Road Car Company.

The Pioneer expands

In 1932, Arthur Mayne had the foresight to lodge an application with the Traffic Commissioner to operate a feeder service from the residential area of Greenside Lane in Droylsden, along Manor Road to Edge Lane. From there, he proposed that passengers could transfer to the firm's Manchester/Audenshaw service, presenting the local community with new links with the City. Naturally, the proposals drew objections from Manchester Corporation and a hearing was arranged for 4th January 1933.

Despite the Corporation's latest attempts to scupper Arthur Mayne's plans, the licence was granted with effect from 21st January, subject to an amended timetable being submitted. Arthur Mayne now had exclusive rights to operate along Manor Road, an area not yet fully developed, that would sow the seeds of the company's fortune. Two years later, the company applied to extend the route along Chappell Road to Medlock Street, a distance of about half a mile. Again the Corporation objected, but the licence was granted from 2nd March 1935.

The first Regents

In any bus and coach fleet there are usually one or two vehicles which have represented a particular landmark in the company's progress. For Maynes, one of the first such occasions occurred in November 1934 when the company introduced the first AEC Regent to the Audenshaw service. The acquisition of this double-decker bus was considered, at the time, to be a concrete expression of Arthur Mayne's rising belief in the value of a standardised fleet of AEC vehicles.

Prior to its unannounced delivery, Manchester Corporation is believed to have tried to have Arthur's licence suspended for running what they considered to be obsolete vehicles. The matter would have been lodged with the Ministry of Transport who eventually dispatched an inspector to investigate the allegation. On the morning of his visit, however, the man from the Ministry would not only find Maynes fleet of dark blue single-decker buses, but the shiny new AEC Regent as well. AXJ496 was said to have been on its first day in service and the staff at Maynes were soon encouraging the inspector to note defects in the Corporation's buses instead.

The Regent was also responsible for introducing a new livery to the bus operation and this would eventually replace the Pioneer livery with colours more similar to that of Maynes Premier Motors. Choosing the new colour scheme had not been easy, for it was not only Maynes coaches that were painted red and cream, so were Manchester Corporation's trams and omnibuses. To avoid any confusion Arthur Mayne decided to paint his buses maroon and turquoise instead. He also decided to have a green light fitted to the front of the bus and

Maynes first double-decker bus poses in Dale Street (near the junction of Oldham Street) as its guard and passengers wait patiently in the rain. AXJ496 was fitted with a petrol engine, which gave a weight advantage and would permit a higher payload on the chassis than its diesel counterpart. The elegant Park Royal bodywork had a sliding front entrance and was originally fitted with 60 seats.

instructed his crews that it should be lit as soon as it went dark in order that his customers could distinguish the firm's buses from those of his arch rival. This method of identification was so successful that it would remain the nocturnal trademark of the family's bus operations for many years to come.

The Audenshaw omnibus route continued to prosper and another AEC Regent (BNF553) was acquired in August 1935 to replace one of the Pioneer single-deckers. The Crossleys had been progressively replaced with the more reliable Dennis E-type single-deckers acquired from Yorkshire Woollen District and these were gradually replaced, in turn, by high capacity double-deckers.

The family's transport business was now well and truly established and Arthur had done much to make his father proud. Not only had he built up a thriving motor coach operation and acquired the goodwill and licences of an equally prosperous omnibus service, but he had two new double-decker buses as well. Sadly, his father would not live to see the venture prosper and develop into the area's principal independent bus and coach operator.

Following the death of his father in 1935, Arthur took the opportunity of registering the business under the Companies Act of 1929 as a Limited Liability Company. On the 13th day of December 1935, the business was officially incorporated as A. Mayne and Son Limited. The registered office of the company was that of the furniture shop at 193/195 Ashton New Road and the directors and shareholders of the company were Arthur and his mother, Matilda Emily Mayne.

Another two Regents were purchased in 1936. These were also fitted with high capacity, Park Royal bodywork, bringing the double-

deck fleet up to four vehicles. Both single-deck and double-deck machines were used on the Audenshaw service with just one single-decker bus providing the feeder service along Manor Road.

In February 1936, Maynes tried to extend their popular Audenshaw service. The motor buses currently terminated on Droylsden Road just past the junction of Kershaw Lane. Arthur's latest proposal called for the bus to turn off the main road and operate along the full length of North Road (now North Drive) to terminate at the junction of Brendon Drive, a distance of about half a mile. He also sought approval to run duplicate journeys where necessary to cater for the increased demand at certain times of the day, but the Commissioner refused to vary the conditions of the licence.

Five months later, Maynes bought their most famous single-decker bus. SM8353 was a little pig-nosed Albion single-decker acquired from United Automobile Services which had its seating capacity reduced to enable one-man operation. After entering service in July 1936, the bus would spend the last three years of its life working the "penny ride" service along Manor Road. With its regular driver Mr Bill Finelow behind the wheel, the Albion was renowned for its speed and reliability and such was its popularity with the passengers they gave it a name – the Flying Pig.

The coaching side expands

Licences to operate express services, excursions and tours previously held by Arthur Mayne were transferred to the new limited liability company in the early part of 1936. When the Blackpool licence for the Stalybridge, Ashton, Audenshaw and Droylsden areas was transferred, it was changed into an express licence, which is what Mr Mayne had originally applied for back in 1930. Despite this change, the company could still only offer the west coast resorts of Lytham, St.Annes and Blackpool as destinations. They could not offer those potential customers the wide variety of destinations available on the excursion and tours licence for the East Manchester area. Maynes tried to remedy this situation in 1938, applying to substitute their express licence in favour of operating their excursion and tours programme

The inside of AXJ496 can be seen clearly in these two pictures taken by Park Royal Vehicles on 30th November 1934. The severe limit on gross weights at the time meant that the Regent was a little austere inside, although the absence of interior lining panels, for example, was not uncommon.

This posed line-up shows the Mayne fleet in the summer of 1937, shortly after the company had taken delivery of four new AEC Regal coaches. The coach nearest the picture (DND5) was added later by the photographer and was in fact one of the newer Regals fitted with a fake registration. This was supposedly carried out for a fifth Regal coach which was still on order. DND5 was never delivered, however, and the order was thought to have been cancelled following the acquisition of Bowkers three year old Regal coach (BNF773) in 1938.

The company acquired two more Regents in 1936. CNB1 was delivered on 9th March 1936 and would be followed six months later by CVR1. Maynes would then have four 62-seat Regents, making Arthur Mayne the proud owner of the highest capacity two-axle buses in the country.

A. MAYNE & SON LTD.
195, ASHTON NEW ROAD.

EASt 0707.
DROylsden 1396.

TIME TABLE.

MONDAYS to FRIDAYS. — Audenshaw to Manchester.

	a.m.	a.m.	a.m.	and EVERY TEN MINUTES to	a.m.	a.m.	then EVERY TWENTY MINUTES to	p.m.	p.m.	and EVERY TEN MINUTES	p.m.	p.m.	then EVERY TWENTY MINUTES to	p.m.	p.m.	a.m.	a.m.	a.m.
KERSHAW LANE, Audenshaw	5 40	6 35	6 57		9 7	9 27		5 7	5 17		6 27	6 47		11 7	11 27	12 30	1 30	2 20
MARKET ST., Droylsden	5 45	6 40	7 0		9 10	9 30		5 10	5 20		6 30	6 50		11 10	11 30	12 35	1 35	TO DEPOT
EDGE LANE, "	5 50	6 45	7 4		9 14	9 34		5 14	5 24		6 34	6 54		11 14	11 34	12 45	1 45	
DALE STREET, Manchester	6 0	6 55	7 17		9 27	9 47		5 27	5 37		6 47	7 7		11 30	11 55	1 0	2 0	

MONDAYS to FRIDAYS. — Manchester to Audenshaw.

	a.m.	a.m.	a.m.	and EVERY TEN MINUTES	a.m.	then EVERY TWENTY MINUTES	p.m.	p.m.	and EVERY TEN MINUTES	p.m.	p.m.	then EVERY TWENTY MINUTES	p.m.	Midnight	a.m.	a.m.
DALE STREET, Manchester	6 0	7 5	7 17		9 27		4 47	4 57		6 27	6 47		11 30	12 0	1 0	2 0
EDGE LANE, Droylsden	6 15	7 18	7 30		9 40		5 0	5 10		6 40	7 0		11 45	12 15	1 15	—
MARKET ST., "	6 25	7 23	7 35		9 45		5 5	5 15		6 45	7 5		11 50	12 20	1 20	—
KERSHAW LANE, Audenshaw	6 30	7 25	7 37		9 47		5 7	5 17		6 47	7 7		11 55	12 30	1 30	2 20 TO DEPOT

SATURDAYS. — Audenshaw to Manchester.

	a.m.	a.m.	a.m.	and EVERY TEN MINUTES to	a.m.	a.m.	then EVERY TWENTY MINUTES to	Noon	p.m.	and EVERY FIFTEEN MINUTES to	p.m.	a.m.	a.m.	a.m.
KERSHAW LANE, Audenshaw	5 40	6 35	6 57		9 7	9 27		12 7	12 25		11 25	12 30	1 30	2 20
MARKET ST., Droylsden	5 45	6 40	7 0		9 10	9 30		12 10	12 27		11 30	12 35	1 35	TO DEPOT
EDGE LANE, "	5 50	6 45	7 4		9 14	9 34		12 14	12 30		11 34	12 45	1 45	
DALE STREET, Manchester	6 0	6 55	7 17		9 27	9 47		12 30	12 45		11 55	1 0	2 0	

SATURDAYS. — Manchester to Audenshaw.

	a.m.	a.m.	a.m.	and EVERY TEN MINUTES to	a.m.	then EVERY TWENTY MINUTES to	Noon	p.m.	p.m.	p.m.	and EVERY FIFTEEN MINUTES to	p.m.	Midnight	a.m.	a.m.
DALE STREET, Manchester	6 0	7 5	7 17		9 27		12 7	12 20	12 30	12 45		11 45	12 0	1 0	2 0
EDGE LANE, Droylsden	6 15	7 18	7 30		9 45		12 20	12 35	12 45	1 5		11 45	12 15	1 15	—
MARKET ST., "	6 25	7 23	7 35		9 45		12 23	12 37	12 50	1 5		11 50	12 20	1 20	—
KERSHAW LANE, Audenshaw	6 30	7 25	7 37		9 47		12 30	12 40	12 55	1 10		11 55	12 30	1 30	2 20 TO DEPOT

SUNDAYS. — Audenshaw to Manchester.

	a.m.	p.m.	p.m.	p.m.	p.m.	p.m.	p.m.	and EVERY FORTY MINUTES to	p.m.	p.m.	p.m.	p.m.	p.m.	p.m.
KERSHAW LANE, Audenshaw	11 30	12 10	12 50	1 30	2 10	2 50	3 30		9 50	10 10	10 30	10 50	11 10	11 30
MARKET ST., Droylsden	11 32	12 12	12 52	1 32	2 12	2 52	3 32		9 52	10 12	10 32	10 52	11 12	11 32
EDGE LANE, "	11 35	12 15	12 55	1 35	2 15	2 55	3 35		9 55	10 15	10 35	10 55	11 15	11 35
DALE STREET, Manchester	11 50	12 30	1 10	1 50	2 30	3 10	3 50		10 10	10 30	10 50	11 10	11 30	TO DEPOT

SUNDAYS. — Manchester to Audenshaw.

	a.m.	p.m.	p.m.	p.m.	p.m.	p.m.	p.m.	and EVERY FORTY MINUTES to	p.m.	p.m.	p.m.	p.m.	p.m.	p.m.
DALE STREET, Manchester	11 50	12 30	1 10	1 50	2 30	3 10	3 50		9 50	10 10	10 30	10 50	11 10	11 30
EDGE LANE, Droylsden	12 5	12 45	1 25	2 5	2 45	3 25	4 5		10 5	10 25	10 45	11 5	11 25	11 45
MARKET ST., "	12 7	12 47	1 27	2 7	2 47	3 27	4 7		10 7	10 27	10 47	11 7	11 27	11 47
KERSHAW LANE, Audenshaw	12 10	12 50	1 30	2 10	2 50	3 30	4 10		10 10	10 30	10 50	11 10	11 30	11 50 TO DEPOT

Printed by Mark Buckley (T.U. 48-hr.) Forms St., Openshaw, M/cr. 11

This timetable for the Audenshaw service was effective from 9th October 1937.

---

from the towns of Stalybridge, Ashton, Audenshaw and Droylsden. Unfortunately, all the other local operators objected to the application and the Traffic Commissioner refused to grant the licences.

The company had been trying to gain licences in the Salford area since the implementation of the Road Traffic Act. In January 1936, attempts were made to take over the licence of Lamb and Whittingslow. At the time, they were operating an express service to Blackpool from their operating base at North Grecian Street, Lower Broughton. As a result of objections from about half a dozen operators, including locally-based J.W. Fieldsend, the application was refused. Maynes now began to look closer to home and on the 8th April 1936, acquired the excursions and tours licence of D. S. Webb, based at 71 Ashton New Road, Beswick. This gave the coaching operation more licences and additional pick-up points in the area.

Three more AEC Regals were purchased in 1937; DNC156, DND3 and DNF2 were all fitted with 32-seat Duple coach bodies and, despite the accelerating drift towards war in Europe, the coaching operation continued to prosper and expand. In July 1938 the tours licence of John Bowker, based at 21 Cross Street, Bradford, Manchester was also acquired. Bowker operated tours to Southport and Blackpool from the Beswick and Bradford areas of the city and was operated as a separate subsidiary (with one vehicle) for a number of years.

All change on Ashton New Road

The licence for the Corporation's Ashton New Road omnibus service (now known as service 6) was renewed in February 1937 and Arthur Mayne appealed against this decision, wanting conditions attached to his rival's licence which would require them to seek his permission to operate duplicates and approve any proposed timetable change. This went to the Minister for Transport, who declined to make an order on the North West Traffic Commissioner.

Maynes revised the times of all its services in 1937. The Droylsden service was modified on Saturdays from 24th July, with permission being granted to operate double-decker buses on the route after 2100 hours. The company could now also operate the service on all Bank Holidays. The Audenshaw service was revised from 9th October, with a ten minute service now operating during the peak, widening to a twenty minute service off-peak and an hourly night service after midnight. On Sundays an approximate 40 minute service was provided throughout most of the day.

The patronage on the Droylsden service continued to grow as the area around Manor Road and Chappell Road was developed. In December 1937, Maynes applied to extend the service from Chappell Road along a new stretch of road which was about to be completed. The company wanted its omnibuses to turn left at the top of Chappell Road and follow the new Sunnyside Road as far as Shrewsbury Road, where buses would turn to come back. They also sought permission to operate double-decker buses when necessary and not just on Saturday evenings. The Commissioner decided to grant the operation of double-deckers when necessary, but decided (at that time), not to allow the extension to Shrewsbury Road.

In January 1938, the company was given permission to operate a football journey to and from Old Trafford or Maine Road on match days, and this was soon followed by the introduction of another two Regents. One of these had recently been acquired from Nottingham City Transport and was sent to Park Royal in 1938 to be rebodied.

The company now had a peak vehicle requirement for eight buses, although four vehicles could do all that was necessary during the quieter times of the day. Figures in respect of passenger journeys during one quarter of 1938 showed a record total of over 500,000 individual journeys were made on the stage carriage services. In addition to extensive contract usage, a further 20,000 passengers were carried on excursions and on the Blackpool express service.

With a relatively small but growing fleet, it was important that no vehicle was off the road for any long period of time, and this was achieved by conducting all maintenance in the company's Queen Street premises and using the spare unit system, so that engines, gearboxes, axles or steering boxes could be changed over complete. Minor body repairs were also carried out by the company. As a result, no Maynes vehicle would be off the road for more than a day.

New premises

With a growing fleet of double-deckers, parking and maintaining the Regents inside the Queen Street premises was now becoming a problem. The roof at the front end of the garage had been altered in 1934 to enable double-deckers to be parked inside, but the Regents could still only gain access to half of the inspection pit. An extension had also been built at the rear to provide storage and office space, but even this was unable to accommodate the needs of firm's twenty-six employees.

A team of ten drivers and their guards now worked out of the depot, many of whom keenly assisted the four mechanics charged with maintaining the fleet. Overseeing the operation was Arthur's brother-in-law, Mr Frank Wade, who acted as both garage foreman and traffic manager. Assisting him was the company inspector who walked for miles each day, ensuring all was well with the company's bus route.

Despite beginning a search for bigger premises, it was decided as a short-term measure to raise the rear section of the garage roof. Arrangements were made so that this would be completed before the ex Nottingham Regent returned from Park Royal and the builders were working towards this when the company despatched a driver to collect it from the bodybuilders.

Unbeknown to the driver, the reconstruction work would take longer than expected, and anyone walking near the company's premises on his return would have seen the gleaming Regent accelerating along Queen Street just before it entered the garage at some considerable speed. They will also have heard a sudden, urgent screech of brakes and an almighty crash as the bus hit the steel beams above the inspection pit. Needless to say Arthur Mayne was none too pleased and promptly opened the driver's pay packet and removed the bonus he was about to give him.

Arthur's search for bigger premises would eventually lead him to the disused dye works and tannery which occupied an area of land alongside Ashton New Road in Clayton. The land had belonged to a wealthy local businessman of German descent who was forced to flee the area during the Great War. His land was eventually bought by Arthur Mayne, who set about converting the tannery building into a garage and workshop. The land at the rear was cleared to provide a parking area for the expanding fleet and a petrol filling station was to be opened alongside the garage forecourt. Completed in 1938, Maynes moved into their present headquarters at 974-998 Ashton New Road during the spring of 1939.

The end of the Ashton New Road trams

Manchester and Ashton Corporations' trams had been operating between Manchester and Ashton via the corridors of Ashton New Road and Ashton Old Road since 1903. Indeed these extensions to the tramway had heralded the end of the horse-drawn tram at the end of March of that year. The first tramway replacement came in 1930, when the 53 route was converted to motor bus operation. Five years later, Manchester's tramways to Middleton, Altrincham and Rochdale were also converted to motor buses. With more than half of its

tramway already abandoned, the City Council urged its Transport Committee to consider the question of trolleybuses, the motives being patriotic (the use of home produced coal for power instead of imported fuel), coupled with a certain amount of civic pride, as other cities also operated trolleybuses.

The Transport Committee, acting under the advice of its general manager, saw no virtue in the trolleybus and decided that the next conversion (Ashton Old Road) should be to motor buses as planned. The trolleybus advocates were not easily dissuaded however and after a struggle in the City Council, it was decided that an experiment should be carried out and the necessary Parliamentary powers were obtained to convert both Ashton Old Road and the parallel Ashton New Road to trolleybus operation.

On the 1st March 1938, the Ashton New Road tram service was curtailed at the Snipe in Audenshaw enabling the first trolleybuses to operate along Ashton Old Road. The last of the Ashton New Road trams ran on 30th July 1938 and a large crowd gathered to watch the historic event.

The trolleybus services which replaced them were also numbered 26 and 27 and ran through to Audenshaw (Snipe) and Stalybridge. Shorter workings were also operated along Ashton New Road as far as Edge Lane in Droylsden and these were numbered 27x. In contrast to the Ashton Old Road services 28 and 29, and like the tramcars before them, the Ashton New Road services were only operated by Manchester Corporation.

Maynes had now seen the disappearance of the tramcar and the arrival of a new form of competitor, which continued to compete with the independent for traffic to Droylsden and Audenshaw. Limited stop service 6, now running between Lower Mosley Street and Glossop, provided an even quicker alternative.

Over the years Manchester Corporation Transport Department would make many determined attempts to take over Mayne's business. In 1938, Arthur Mayne came close to selling the company after Manchester Corporation offered him £31,000 for his fleet of buses and coaches. Only at the last moment did a change of heart compel him to decline the offer. Many more take-over attempts would follow, but Maynes were to resist them all and remain independent. On one occasion, as Maynes and myth would forever have it, the Corporation's General Manager is reputed to have approached Arthur to make an offer for his business. Mr Mayne apparently replied that this was indeed a coincidence, as he was thinking of making an offer for theirs.

Arthur Mayne seen is his Special Constable's uniform. Specials were know as Commandants in those days and Arthur was based at the local Mill Street Police Station.

Chapter Three

Shortages

The outbreak of war in September 1939 brought Maynes summer season to an abrupt halt and the holiday services were terminated early. Three of the coaches were soon commandeered for the war effort, ironically by the very same man who had sold them the vehicles just a few years earlier. Long distance coach services were re-instated a few months later, only to be suspended again from 30th September 1942.

Due to his age and general health, Arthur Mayne was unable to be conscripted for military service. He would however continue to serve the local community as a Special Constable for the area. This was a task which he enjoyed tremendously and would continue to do even after the war. Under the management of Frank Wade, Maynes would also continue to serve the community, running their local bus services to Droylsden and Audenshaw.

The hostilities would make the operation of bus services extremely difficult with staff shortages, fuel rationing, the blackout and air raids. In the preceding months detailed plans had been made to deal with the effects of war, with operators submitting plans to the Traffic Commissioners detailing bus service provisions requiring only 60% of the current fuel consumption. Maynes are believed to have reduced their services to peak hour and evening work, therefore limiting fuel consumption to the absolute minimum.

The Certificate of Fitness test which all motor buses were subject to was suspended, but the shortage of vehicle spares meant that even the most basic of maintenance tasks became difficult. Whilst this reduced maintenance costs in the short term, it meant buses gradually became unserviceable as the few remaining mechanics struggled to keep them running.

Blackout conditions reduced demand and placed a heavy burden on the platform staff, most of whom were women. Buses also had their interior lighting reduced and the conductors were issued with shaded battery lamps, by the light of which they collected the fares and issued the tickets.

Driving the Regents was no easy task either, as the restrictions on vehicle lighting also made it a requirement to mask all side and headlamps, and the familiar green light fitted to the fronts of the Regents was extinguished. Despite a government directive to paint white bands on the edges of mudguards and rear corners of vehicles, driving

in the dark was both unpleasant and dangerous. In fact from 1939 to August 1940 blackout accidents would claim more lives than enemy bombs.

By the middle of June 1940, German troops had occupied Paris and the French had surrendered. Britain, separated from the dreaded Wehmacht by just 26 miles of water, prepared itself for invasion. To confuse the enemy, road signs were removed and for some months Maynes Regents ran without displaying any form of destination. This was not a problem on a summer evening but on a dark winter night the company's passengers would have little means of establishing whether the approaching bus was a Mayne Regent or Corporation Crossley.

The winter of 1940/1 was bitterly cold and much of the country was submerged under several inches of snow during the last two weeks of January. On one occasion, a severe frost resulted in large amounts of ice accumulating on the overhead wires and this effectively confined the municipal trolleybuses to their garages the following morning. Maynes, always prepared to lend a helping hand to an operator in need, actively co-operated with their rivals in a determined attempt to get the travelling public to their destinations.

One month after the Allies invaded Normandy, another independent operator left the stage carriage arena. Holt Brothers of

FJ7821 was acquired in 1938 from Exeter and was originally fitted with Brush bodywork. It was re-bodied in 1942 by East Lancs and, as supplies of maroon paint were restricted, the Regent is seen here in its wartime grey livery. Some of the Park Royal Regents were also rebodied by East Lancs after the war.

Rochdale, better known as Yelloway, sold its Manchester to Rochdale bus route to the surrounding municipalities in July 1944, predicting a great opportunity for long distance coach services when the war was over.

The end of the war would result in the gradual easing of restrictions. With little or no private fuel there was an increased demand for Maynes bus and coach services, creating an insatiable call on the company's resources, which showed little sign of declining in the coming years.

The post-war years

With the Certificate of Fitness re-imposed for motor buses there were major arrears in maintenance. Limited company resources concentrated on mechanical spares, but these were costly and in short supply, as the government placed an emphasis on exports. To solve the immediate problem, it was decided that another Regent bus would be purchased and cannibalised for the necessary parts. This was done

in September 1945, when a fourteen year old Regent was acquired from Nottingham City Transport. Another would be acquired from the same source eight months later.

The company was also experiencing staffing problems and, in stark contrast to Manchester Corporation, retained the services of its female 'clippies' even after the war. With the eventual relaxing of fuel restrictions, Maynes restored the off-peak and Sunday workings on their bus services and a degree of normality returned.

In the Manchester Corporation Act of 1946 there was a section entitled 'Trolley Vehicle Powers' which sought powers to construct a trolleybus route along Manor Road to Sunnyside Road in Droylsden. This went to the House of Lords who ruled that MCTD could not operate on Manor Road without the agreement of A. Mayne & Son Ltd. This was a remarkable victory for the independent and on returning from the House of Lords, Arthur Mayne took Olive Brien, a friend of the family, out to celebrate. They were married a few months later on the 4th July 1946.

JNC4 was a Bellhouse Hartwell-bodied AEC Regal III, and the last of a batch of six Regals delivered to the company after the war. The coach was delivered in 1948 and is seen, shortly before its withdrawal in December 1960, carrying the fleet number 16.

This AEC Regent Mark III was one of two delivered in 1949 which were the first Mayne vehicles to be equipped with semi-automatic gearboxes. KNA877 sits at the company's terminus in Dale Street, Manchester, and is just about to load up for its return journey to Audenshaw.

Families re-united for the first time in years were now beginning to pick up the threads of their lives once again and this, coupled with the glorious summer of 1946, created long queues as the company struggled to shift the crowds of holiday-makers with an aged fleet of coaches. Two new AEC Regal coaches helped lessen the burden and in February 1947, it was announced that these two vehicles (HNE2/3) formed part of an order for six Regals and two Regent double-deckers.

The latest Regal coach chassis (the mark III) was primarily intended for overseas markets in both left and right-hand drive form. Some were later released onto the home market with initial sales going to many vehicle-starved independent coach operators such as A. Mayne & Son. HXJ566/7 arrived in time for the 1947 season and were soon joined by the company's first Duple-bodied Bedford. HNE512 had coach seating for 29 passengers and would be followed by a repeat order in 1948. As it had not been possible to buy new coaches in 1945, Mayne's very first Bedford had been an SMT-bodied bus which was fitted with padded seating for coach work.

Despite a notoriously bad winter, mother nature attempted to make amends with a long spell of glorious sunshine during the summer months of 1948. Demand for Maynes express and excursion operations was greater than ever that season and the remaining two Bellhouse Hartwell-bodied Regals (JNC3/4) were quickly pressed into service alongside another new Bedford OB (JND404). A surprise delivery in 1949 was a Burlingham-bodied Leyland Tiger PS2, the first Leyland to enter service with the company in eighteen years. KVM729 joined KNA876 and KNA877, the two new Regent III double-deckers, fitted with 59-seat East Lancs bodywork.

The not-so-thrifty 'fifties

The increasing costs of labour, vehicles, spares and fuel were absorbed by the post-war boom until the end of the 1940s. When the boom tailed off, however, and passenger numbers began to fall as a result of increased personal transport, those spiralling costs became more and more evident against a canvas of declining profitability.

Maynes bus and coach fleet was by now heavily standardised on AEC, with the bus fleet based exclusively on the Regent double-decker. The company's coach-buying policy had largely been in favour of the AEC Regal during the firm's first twenty years. Now, however, that policy was undergoing a subtle change. Another Duple-bodied Bedford OB joined the fleet in 1950 and was followed by similar machines throughout the 1950s.

Their first underfloor-engined coaches arrived in January 1954, having been acquired from Stewart of Glasgow and Broadhead of Dewsbury. The AEC Regal IVs had centre-entrance coach bodies, and were fitted with pre-selective gearboxes and air-pressure brakes. Fuel consumption on these vehicles was heavy by contemporary standards and this no doubt influenced the company's vehicle-buying policy at a time when much attention was paid to fuel economy and reductions in operating costs.

Following the takeover of the Droylsden excursion and tours licence belonging to Shipleys of Ashton-under-Lyne in January 1953, the company began to look at expanding the catchment area for its excursions and tours programme. Expansion through natural growth was slow and often blocked by other operators in the area. The only real way forward was to acquire those neighbouring operators, one by one.

F. & H. Dean Ltd

In March 1957, Maynes acquired the business of F. & H. Dean of Newton Heath along with a fleet of six coaches consisting of four Leylands and two Bedfords. All but one were delivered new to the company, with the only second-hand example leaving the fleet in April 1958. Operated as a separate concern, the five remaining coaches were used until 1961, when Maynes vehicles progressively entered the fleet.

Further takeovers

Another operator running in the midst of Maynes operating area, was S. & H. Barton, based at 72 Blackrock Street, Manchester 11. Trading as Barton Tours, the company held an excursions and tours licence with picking up rights in Ashton-under-Lyne, and this was subsequently acquired by Maynes on 18th September 1957 and added to their existing licences for Stalybridge, Droylsden and East Manchester.

Next came the excursions and tours licences belonging to A. Lea of 6 Westbourne Road, Denton which were taken over from 26th October 1958. Lea operated a Burlingham-bodied Leyland TS1 alongside a Duple-bodied Bedford and a 33-seat Seddon. All three were included in the sale, although the Seddon (which was painted into Maynes red and cream livery) was never actually used by the company.

Another local coach operator was Empress Coaches of 19 Cash Street, Miles Platting. Mr Stubbs, the firm's proprietor, is understood to have turned to Maynes to garage his early model AEC Regal after his premises were demolished in the mid-'fifties. A short time later in March 1959, Stubbs sold the vehicle to Maynes and went into the taxi business instead.

One of the first underfloor-engined coaches to join the fleet came from Broadhead of Dewsbury. HD9304 was an AEC Regal IV and the first Plaxton-bodied vehicle to enter the fleet. The coach is seen in London in the late 1950s.

Three vehicles were acquired from Lea of Denton in October 1958, one of which was a Duple-bodied Bedford SBG. SVM407 was new to Lea in April 1956 and is seen in Southport. It was withdrawn by Maynes in 1963.

A batch of five Duple-bodied Bedford SB1s was delivered to Mayne in February and March 1959. One immediately joined the Dean fleet and was followed three years later by XNB16.

ATJ 511 was acquired from Empress Coaches in March 1959. The twenty-three years old AEC Regal had been rebodied by Plaxton in 1949 and is parked next to a Leyland PS1 belonging to another local coach operator, Edith Morby & Son of Droylsden.

Above: The trusty Bedford SB. 9086ND is a Plaxton Embassy 41-seater which was delivered in April 1962. It was withdrawn in December 1968, to make way for the Bristol LHLs. Note the "M" on the headrest covers.

A batch of four Bedford SBs was delivered in 1963. 2494VM had the later Embassy II coachwork with the slightly restyled front.

The 30th Bedford to enter the fleet was DBU646C, an SB5 with Plaxton Panorama coachwork, which was new to Mayne in June 1965. It is seen on a private hire outside Robertsons Jam factory, Droylsden's world-famous export.

The Mayne coach fleet now comprised nine front-engined Bedford SBs, five front-engined AEC Regals, two underfloor-engined Regal IVs, and a newly-acquired AEC Reliance from the Yelloway fleet. The Dean subsidiary had a further three Bedford SBs and an equal number of Burlingham-bodied Leylands. Fleet numbers were now allocated to the Mayne coach fleet with numbers 1 to 17 being issued in early 1959. No attempt was made at matching the numbers to the vehicles' registration, however, and the whole process was quietly abandoned after the delivery of two Duple-bodied Bedford SBs in 1960.

Four years later, the company's thirst for expansion was quenched through a further spate of licence acquisitions which claimed P. & W. Prestwich of Audenshaw, Shipleys of Ashton, and Claribel Motors of Ardwick. P. & W. Prestwich were originally based at 7 Rosina Street, Higher Openshaw before moving into the neighbouring town of Audenshaw. On 1st May 1964 the Traffic Commissioners granted Maynes application to take over the Prestwichs' licence, giving them picking up rights in Higher Openshaw. Nearly a year later, the company took over the remaining licences belonging to E. Shipley of 10 Henry Square, Ashton. This gave them office accomodation in Ashton town centre – as well as a more central pick-up location – and rights to operate excursions and tours from the town of Mossley.

One of the most fondly remembered coach operators of this period was Claribel, a company which had taken its name from the street in Ardwick in which it was based. On 12th May 1967, Maynes took over the company's excursion and tours licences, gaining picking up rights in the Manchester suburb of Ardwick and additional rights in both Gorton and Stalybridge.

Maynes Buses 1950-69

Maynes spent the early 'fifties acquiring good quality second-hand Regents from the municipal fleets of Leeds, Salford, and Glasgow, and by the end of the decade had amassed around a dozen double-deckers. Of these, four were required to operate the Audenshaw service with a further two employed on Manor Road. The remainder would be used on the company's extensive contract operations.

In 1950 Manchester Corporation renumbered all its trolleybus services into the 210 to 219 group of numbers and thoughts of replacing them all with motor buses began to take root. Only the very

Below left: Two Regents were acquired from Leeds in 1950. AUM434 was numbered 191 in the municipal operator's fleet and is basking in the sunshine on the forecourt of Maynes garage. The blackboards propped up against the unidentified Bedford are announcing afteroon departures to Chester, Chester Zoo and Southport. An evening drive around Cheshire is also being offered.

Below right: This ex Salford Regent was one of two acquired in 1950/1. Only RJ8728 entered service however and the bus is seen loading up at the bottom of Manor Road in preparation for its return trip to the Sunnyside Road estate.

Bottom left: Former London STL1684 was built in 1936 and the combination of the lively 7.7 litre AEC engine and a pre-selective gearbox, produced a nimble bus that was easy to drive. It was fitted with the standard London Passenger Transport Board body and was acquired by Maynes in 1952. It was twenty years old when it was scrapped for spares in 1956.

Bottom right: CUS814 was the last of a batch of three Regents acquired from Glasgow in the 1950s. This Weymann-bodied bus is seen in Audenshaw on the 5th August 1957.

Top left: In September 1954, the company purchased another lightweight AEC Regent III. This time, the one year old bus was a former demonstrator, which arrived in the livery of the City of Oxford Motor Services. As this was somewhat similar to the Mayne bus livery, 7194H would remain in these colours throughout its stay with the company. It was withdrawn in October 1972.

Top right: Another Weymann-bodied Regent II was purchased in 1960. ECY874 had previously seen service in South Wales and was the last second-hand Regent to be purchased.

Upper left: With the early Regents ready for retirement, Maynes placed an order for three new 30ft long Regent Vs for bodying by Park Royal. The Regent V had a vertical 9.6 litre engine similar to that used in AEC's new Reliance coach model. UNF10-2 were delivered in July 1957 and initially restricted to the Audenshaw route.

Upper right: GUF678 was an ex Southdown Leyland Titan PD1, fitted with 54-seat Park Royal bodywork of the 'relaxed utility type'.

Left: Private hire and contract work made up a large proportion of the duties carried out by the Regents. FT5711 is Weymann-bodied Regent II acquired from Tynemouth and is seen on a rare visit to the Salford Corporation terminus at Victoria Bus Station.

high fuel tax, which bus operators were campaigning against, made it economical to keep them running. Thus, Ashton New Road would keep its trolleybuses and services 27 and 26 would become known as the 215 and 216.

Rationing finally ended in 1954, although a dispute with Egypt over the Sudan and the Suez Canal (which had been going on since 1950), meant that restrictions were re-imposed on fuel and oil. With escalating costs and a declining number of passengers, fare increases became the norm throughout the 'fifties. All fare revisions had to be approved by the Traffic Commissioners and justifying such an increase was no easy task, as it required the operator to lay bare his

accounts at a Public Enquiry. As Maynes competed with the co-ordinated services of Manchester, Ashton, SHMD and North Western for traffic in Audenshaw, Droylsden, and Manchester, the company often had to wait for the bigger operators to take the lead in any fare increase.

Service 46

By the early-'fifties the company's Manor Road service was terminating on Sunnyside Road at the junction of Springfield Road, where the Regents would reverse and load up for the short journey back to Manor Road and Edge Lane.

Lancs were now some twenty years old and approaching the end of their working lives. They were finally retired in 1959 after clocking up more than twenty years of loyal and reliable service. No sooner had they departed, when something rather odd occurred.

Maynes' bus fleet, an exclusive home to the Regent for the last twenty-five years suddenly received a Leyland Titan PD1. After GUF678 was overhauled at S. H. Bond in Wythenshawe, consideration was given to buying two more PD1s. The bus was not popular with the road staff, however, as its crash gearbox made it difficult for the uninitiated to drive. No further PD1s would be purchased as a result of this and, after its withdrawal in November 1965, the bus fleet would become exclusively AEC Regent once again.

Having approved the increase in the width of buses to 8ft some ten years earlier, the Ministry of Transport now approved the increase in the length of double-deck buses to 30 feet in 1956, bringing it in line with single-deck vehicles. Maynes' first 30ft long buses would consist of three AEC Regent Vs which were bodied by Park Royal and delivered in July 1957. As it was considered too difficult to reverse them on Sunnyside Road, UNF10-12 were initially restricted to the Audenshaw route, being joined by three similar machines (6972-4ND) at the end of 1961. Service 46 was in operation by this time and, as buses now operated in a loop around the estate, the problem of reversing them had been solved.

Another two Regent Vs were delivered in January 1964. This time 8859/60VR had bodywork by East Lancs and were followed, just over a year later, by CXJ520-2C which had bodywork by Neepsend, an East Lancs associate. This batch of vehicles would turn out to be the last of Maynes' AEC Regents and entered service in August 1965, some three years before the type finally ceased production.

The majority of passengers were heading into the city and the transfer at Edge Lane was cumbersome and would do little to discourage people from making the journey by motor car, if the opportunity arose. The solution to the problem lay in extending the service along Ashton New Road to Manchester. As this would require the agreement of Manchester Corporation, the independent approached the City's Transport Department with a view to operating a joint service between Sunnyside Road and Manchester (Stevenson Square).

The agreement made in January 1958, called for the provision of two Mayne AEC Regents and one bus from the Corporation's Hyde Road Garage. A further three vehicles were required at peak times and these would be provided by the Corporation during the summer and Maynes during the winter.

Commencing on 2nd July 1958, new limited stop service 46 served the full length of Sunnyside Road (terminating at the junction with Lancaster Road), as well as serving Greenside Lane and Springfield Road. The family concern now had two routes into the city, with the Audenshaw service continuing to terminate on Dale Street.

Last of the half-cabs

The early model Regents, having been re-bodied in mid-life by East

An agreement is reached

When Ralph Bennett, the new General Manager, took control of Manchester Corporation's Transport Department in April 1965, one of the first proposals he made was to replace the trolleybuses. As Maynes was the only other licenced operator of a stopping motor bus service on Ashton New Road it was in a strong tactical position to object to the municipal's plans. The last time the Corporation sought Maynes agreement was back in 1946 when Manchester wanted to construct a trolleybus route along Manor Road.

Manchester was determined on this occasion that approval be obtained to replace all the trolleybus routes with motor buses. They had, after all, never wanted them in the first place and did not want the embarrassment of being stuck with the Ashton New Road route. Maynes on the other hand, did not want any more motor bus routes competing with its long established Kershaw Lane and Manor Road routes.

Negotiations were entered into and an agreement made on 7th December 1966. The Kershaw Lane service which ran parallel to the 215 and 216 would be taken over by the Corporation and incorporated into a new service 214. In exchange, Maynes would then run all the mileage on the 46 and retain 85% of the revenue. The remaining 15% (less 15% of the running costs) would be paid to the newly-titled City Transport Department every quarter.

The trolleybuses ran for the last time on Friday 30th December 1966, but there would be no formal ceremonies. On the following day Maynes operated their Audenshaw service for the last time, ending nearly forty years of independent operation on the route. After the New Year the company would begin their exclusive operation of the 46 and Manchester City Transport would start their peak hour service 214 between Audenshaw (Ryecroft Hall) and Manchester (Piccadilly).

From 8th July 1968, Manchester City Transport reorganised its services in the Droylsden area. Some of the short workings on the 216 to Audenshaw were diverted via North Road and Edge Lane to form new service 217, whilst the former trolleybus route 215, which now terminated at Edge Lane, was extended to Clayton Bridge. To complete the reorganisation service 46 became the 213.

Into SELNEC

In the 1964 General Election the Labour Party returned to power again under Harold Wilson and in 1966 they increased their majority for a second term. Labour was very much committed to an integrated transport system and appointed the Rt. Hon. Mrs Barbara Castle MP as Minister for Transport. Various Government White Papers were produced until the final White Paper 'Urban Passenger Transport' was implemented under the Transport Act 1968.

Under the provisions of the Act, the nationalised Transport Holding Company and privately-controlled BET companies and the independent West Riding company were brought together to form the National Bus Company. Passenger Transport Executives were created in the metropolitan areas and these were given powers to acquire the municipal and private bus operators within their regional boundaries.

The South East Lancashire and North East Cheshire Passenger Transport Executive came into being on the 1st September 1969. When operations commenced two months later, SELNEC had acquired the municipal bus undertakings of Ashton, Bolton, Bury, Leigh,

Manchester, Oldham, Ramsbottom, Rochdale, Salford, SHMD and Stockport. The PTE would also go on to acquire the local operations of North Western and the Wigan municipality, and became the first PTE to conclude an operating agreement with British Rail.

Further attempts would be made to acquire A. Mayne & Son Ltd, but the family held together and politely declined each offer. Following the death of his mother in 1957, Arthur's wife Olive had taken on the role of company secretary and the couple had welcomed their oldest son, Andrew, to the board in 1968. His younger brother, Stephen, would join them three years later upon reaching the age of 21.

It was Stephen Mayne's continuing interest and eventual wish to work in the business that kept the family from selling to SELNEC and one of the main reasons why the company would remain independent. Even though the Road Service Licence for the 213 had passed with the acquisition of Manchester City Transport to SELNEC PTE, Maynes continued to be protected by the agreement they had made with Manchester Corporation.

GMT is born

Under the local Government reorganisation plan on 1st April 1974, responsibility for public transport passed to the Transportation Committee of the newly formed Greater Manchester Council. SELNEC PTE then changed its name to Greater Manchester Transport and the neighbouring bus undertaking of Wigan Corporation was acquired.

GMTs peak hour service 214 continued to run between Audenshaw and Manchester and would be merged into service 216 by November of 1975. Two months later Greater Manchester Transport acquired Lancashire United Transport, the biggest private bus undertaking in Britain. This meant that there was only one private bus operator left in the whole of Greater Manchester.

Maynes still quietly going about its business had outlived all the private and municipal bus undertakings and withstood all the attempts to put an end to the company's activities. Maynes had been operating bus services along Ashton New Road for nearly fifty years and was now on its third generation of AEC Regent buses.

Below left: Another two Regent Vs were delivered in January 1964. 8859VR has bodywork by East Lancs.
Below right: The last of Maynes AEC Regents entered service in August 1965. CXJ520-2C were fitted with air brakes and for many months the drivers struggled to get used to this new system of braking. One driver, concerned about the comfort of his passengers, was told the buses would stop better if he drove in his stocking feet. This he duly did until it was realised the mechanic had only been joking. CXJ522C is seen on the last day of the Audenshaw service.

Chapter Four
Maynes Coaches – The Underfloor Era

Mayne's first Bedford vehicle had arrived in 1945. Six years later, the Dunstable-based manufacturer launched the 40-seat, front-engined SB chassis. Up until this time, the fleet had consisted of vehicles mostly of AEC parentage, with around sixteen Regal coaches and a dozen Regent buses, not forgetting of course an early AEC Reliance. Only three faithful Bedfords had been granted an appearance.

By the late sixties, however, the tables had been turned and one could count the number of AEC coaches in the fleet on the fingers of just one hand. The trusty Bedford now reigned supreme, with thirty SB-type coaches having entered the fleet since its launch in 1950. The first of the much larger 52-seat VAL series coaches entered service in 1965, followed two years later by the smaller (45-seat) VAM. Other chassis types purchased by the company included the AEC Reliance and the Bristol LH.

Maynes last AECs and first Bristols

The AEC Reliance was one of the longest-lived underfloor-engined single-deckers on the market and was produced at AEC's Southhall factory between 1953 and 1979. Maynes purchased their first Reliance coach from Holt Brothers of Oldham in 1959, whilst their second was purchased practically new in 1963, after a brief spell as a demonstrator for Lancashire Motor Traders. In 1972, Maynes purchased four dual-purpose Reliances which were fitted with bus grant doors and painted into the maroon and turquoise bus livery. When new, FBU302-5K were regular evening and Sunday performers on the 213 service. However, the route's busy nature and the fact that it was crew operated meant that these vehicles were not well suited for use on stage carriage work. They spent most of their working life with the company on coaching duties and the last Reliance was withdrawn in December 1980.

The Bristol LH had a shorter lifespan than the AEC Reliance. Launched in 1967, the horizontal-engined Bristol LH was originally developed as a 9.2m lightweight single-decker. Its bigger, 11m long counterpart was known as the LHL. Maynes bought five LHs, all of

The Plaxton VAL with its very-sixties rear-end.

ENE454D was one of two Bedford VALs delivered in 1966. They would be followed in 1967 by six of the smaller 45-seater Bedford VAMs.

which were fitted with Leyland 400 engines and carried Plaxton's Panorama coachwork. The first three (TBU7-9G) were LHLs fitted with 51 seats, whilst the last two (WBU714/5H) were built on the shorter wheelbase and fitted with 45 seats. They were withdrawn in 1980.

R. Connolly Ltd, Gorton.

In 1971, Maynes applied to the Traffic Commissioner to take over the excursions and tours licences of Connollys of Gorton, who had long been a rival to Arthur Mayne's operation. Finally, on the 22nd October 1971, the business, licences and remaining Plaxton-bodied Bedford VAL coach passed to the rival family concern.

End of the road for
Dean of Newton Heath

The remaining vehicles acquired with the operation of F. & H. Dean were gradually replaced during 1961 with coaches from the Mayne fleet. Strangely, it was the Bedfords that were the first to go, being replaced by two AEC Regals. HNE2/3 were purchased by Arthur Mayne in 1946 and originally had bodywork by the Wigan-based Santus company. They were re-bodied by Yeates in 1954 to seat 39 and were transferred to the Dean fleet in 1961.

The three Burlingham-bodied Leylands went at the end of the season and were replaced in time for the next by just one Bedford from the Mayne fleet. Dean of Newton Heath now had three Duple-bodied Bedfords and one Regal. The latter was finally replaced in 1962 by a Plaxton-bodied Bedford and this was followed by similar machines in both 1964 and 1965. No further vehicles were added to the fleet and the six vehicles were gradually phased out after Dean's operating licence was merged with that of A. Mayne & Son from 17th November 1967.

E. Morby & Sons, Ltd of Droylsden

Edith Morby ran her excursions and tours business from 417 Manchester Road, Droylsden, less than half a mile away from Mayne's garage on Ashton New Road. Unlike Arthur Mayne, Mrs Morby was originally licenced to operate excursions from the

Droylsden area and began operations with a 26-seat Albion coach in March 1936. The firm grew slowly over the next thirty years and had a fleet strength of three vehicles throughout the 1960s. A decade later, Morbys were operating two Bedfords when the business was sold to Arthur Mayne as a going concern in 1974. The remaining coaches were operated separately until the licence was merged with that of Maynes in 1976.

Wilson's of Droylsden

The last operator to be acquired by Maynes was Wilson's of Failsworth, which operated excursions and tours from both Failsworth and Droylsden. Having acquired a 12-seater Ford Transit from the company in December 1974, Maynes returned in the spring of 1976 to take over their remaining excursions and tours licence and a 53-seat Ford R226, which was operated until the end of the season. The company's excursion catchment area now encompassed the towns of Ashton-under-Lyne, Audenshaw, Beswick, Blackley, Clayton, Denton, Droylsden, Dukinfield, Failsworth, Gorton, Hyde, Manchester, Miles Platting, Mossley, Moston, Newton Heath, Openshaw and Stalybridge.

Excursions, Tours & Private Hire

By 1978, the coach fleet had been largely standardised on the Bedford chassis with coachwork by Plaxton, and consisted of six 41-seat SBs, four 53-seat YRTs and six 53-seat YMTs. In addition, there were four AEC Reliances and two Bristol LHLs, all with Plaxton coachwork, as well as a 12-seat Ford Transit. The 23-strong coaching fleet was kept busy operating a large number of works and school contracts throughout the working week and was available for express and excursion operations at the weekends.

The company's excursion programme now covered a wide range of destinations with regular departures to Blackpool, Rhyl,

The first AEC Reliance to enter service with Maynes was LBU321, which had centre-entrance Burlingham Seagull coachwork.

63DBU was a Lancashire Motor Traders demonstrator until it was purchased by Arthur Mayne in March 1963.

Four AEC Reliances were delivered in May 1972. Painted in the company's maroon and turquoise bus livery, they had Plaxton Elite Express II coach work and were fitted with bus grant doors. FBU305K is seen in Stevenson Square, operating service 213.

Above: Maynes operated five Bristol LH coaches throughout the seventies. TBU8G had seating for 51, while WBU714H was a 45 seater. Both are seen in Blackpool, preparing for their return to Manchester.

Right: The lightweight Bedford coach range gained the underfloor, 8.3 litre Y-series engines from 1970. Two of the 10 metre long YRQs were already in the fleet when a further two were acquired in 1972. FBU300K is parked next to GNF816E, a Bedford VAM.

Four Bedford SB5s were delivered in March and May of 1973. LBU701-4L were fitted with Plaxton Panorama coachwork and were the first coaches to carry the Mayne fleet name on their sides in bold red lettering.

Scarborough and York. Even in the late 'seventies, Blackpool remained by far the most popular destination for the company's clientele. From the Spring Bank Holiday until the end of September the daily operation to this west coast resort continued, rising to nine or ten vehicles a day at peak periods. The Edinburgh Tattoo was also a popular feature of the excursion programmes around this time.

Despite a gradual fall in fares, the operation of excursions was now a declining market. As this represented a very valuable part of the family business, Maynes had to take positive steps to maintain their existing traffic whilst actively encouraging new growth. The excursion programme had been suffering from the very same factors that were affecting their bus service. With rising unemployment, there was a general reduction in the amount of disposable income, particularly in inner-city areas such as Clayton. Secondly, much of the company's local catchment area was undergoing redevelopment, with demolition of row upon row of terraced dwellings throughout East Manchester.

The long-term prospects were considered to be much better, however, with the gradual redevelopment of the surrounding area. Future growth was seen to be in private hire, weekend breaks and possibly continental tour operations. A more professional approach to marketing the company and its excursions and tours was thought to be needed, with programmes specially designed to offer customers that little bit 'extra' in incentives.

Above: A more striking application of the red and cream livery, enabled the company's new marketing slogan to be carried to good effect on this 1978 Bedford YMT.

Opposite page: The buses made it to Blackpool too. Regent Vs UNF11 and UNF10 are seen at the resort in the upper photograph when new in 1957. Twenty-one years later two of the Bristol VRs rest in Lytham on a damp summers evening.

Chapter Five
Rear-Engined Buses

Eight years after receiving the last of a long line of AEC Regents, Maynes placed an order for five Daimler Fleetlines. The operator's first rear-engined buses would be fitted with Gardner engines and receive bodywork by Charles H. Roe of the Crossgates Carriage Works in Leeds. Roe was now a member of the nationalised Leyland Group and, throughout the early 'seventies, demand for its products was extremely high. Despite placing the order in 1973, the vehicles would not be ready for delivery until June of 1976, when all five finally entered service on the company's bus route.

The timetable for the 213 had remained unchanged for many years and had been built around the needs of the local mill workers who worked a five-and-a half-day week. The gradual reduction in the working week had by then, however, eradicated the need for additional Saturday journeys and the standard fifteen-minute daytime frequency would soon be adopted.

Eleven crews were employed on the service and despite the introduction of the Fleetlines, the company remained a staunch believer in the crew-operated bus. With the fleet equally divided between front and rear entrance buses, the company began to look at replacing the last of its Regent double-deckers. Maynes initial choice would have been a repeat order for the Daimler Fleetline, but a massive order by London Transport for its DMS fleet meant that Daimler had a full order book for the next two years.

The company wanted the vehicles to be fitted with Gardner engines and so the Bristol VR became the only remaining choice. The VR was the last of the first generation of rear-engined double-deck buses to be launched and was developed primarily for the state-owned sector. Fitted with fully automatic transmissions and equipped with semi-coach seating, VJA665-7S replaced the three Neepsend-bodied Regents. The remaining two Regents – which had bodywork by East Lancs – would soldier on into the next decade, acting as spare buses until the company purchased two more Bristols in 1980. They were then loaned to Stevensons of Uttoxeter who ultimately purchased 8860VR. Its sister vehicle 8859VR returned to Manchester for further service and was finally retired in November 1980, signalling the end of the Regent era.

The Roe-bodied Fleetlines were the company's first rear-engined buses acquired at a cost of £25,000 each. LRJ214P is posed outside the Roe factory in Leeds, prior to its journey to Clayton.

Above: Unlike GMT, Maynes used multi-coloured destination blinds throughout the 1980s. When service 209 was introduced the route indicator for the 213 changed from the more usual white lettering on a black background to black lettering on a yellow background. The 209 route indicator initially had blue lettering on a white background (as seen here), but the colours were soon transposed.

Top left: The Bristol VRs had coach seating and were painted in the company's red and cream coach livery. VJA665S is seen off-route on St Andrews Street, Ancoats in 1978.

Left: A further two Bristol VRs were collected from Lowestoft in July 1980, entering service on 1st August.

Service 209: The Lumb Link

Since the closure of Droylsden Railway Station, the residents of the nearby village of Littlemoss had been campaigning for a bus service into Manchester. At the time the area was served by GMT's service 335 (originally Ashton's number 5) which ran from Smallshaw to Droylsden via Ashton, Taunton and Littlemoss. Many of the Littlemoss residents worked or shopped in Manchester – a journey which would involve changing buses in Droylsden.

In the General Election of 1979 the Conservatives returned to office under Mrs Thatcher. It was also the year Maynes launched their first new bus route since the creation of the Sunnyside Road service some forty years earlier. Licenced as a joint service between GMT and Maynes, service 209 was launched on 17th December 1979 and followed the 213 route from Stevenson Square to Chappell Road. From there it operated via Medlock Street and Moorside Street to Littlemoss, Lumb Mill. It was marketed as the Lumb Link and, like service 213, Maynes operated all the mileage on the route.

Greater Manchester Transport then sought Maynes approval to extend their 346 service from Ashton to Droylsden via Taunton and Littlemoss. Agreement between the two operators was reached on the 20th June 1980, subject to before and after surveys which would be designed to measure the effect of this extension on Maynes loadings. The before survey was carried out in the early weeks of July 1980 and, on the 27th of that month, GMT finally penetrated the Sunnyside Road estate with the extension of the 346, operating between Droylsden and Newton (near Hyde).

It was now Maynes turn to seek GMT's approval for the extension of service 209. The frequency on the hourly service had already been stepped up (from March 1980) to every 30 minutes and the company was now seeking to extend the service to serve Hartshead, a large housing estate on the fringe of Ashton-under-Lyne. The extension was agreed by both parties on 28th November and service 209 was extended via Daisy Nook and Waterloo to Hartshead (Pegs Lantern) eight days later.

As this new chapter in the company's stage carriage services began to unfold, another sadly came to a close. Arthur Mayne, now 85 years old, had guided the company's fortunes for the last sixty years, steadily developing it from a fledgling delivery company into the area's principal independent bus and coach operator.

Arthur lived for his family, his church and his business. His death on the 11th November 1980 dealt a sad blow to the company at a time when it was suffering in a changing social and economic climate. Often the loss of a founding generation can lead to a company falling by the wayside, but Arthur and his company were fortunate that his youngest son, Stephen, was capable of taking up the challenge and has continued to take the company forward during the years he has been Managing Director.

Low fares and one-man operation

Despite the continuing profitability of the company's two stage carriage services, operating costs continued to escalate as the company's strong belief in the crew operated bus began to wither. Bus

fares had increased every year from 1975 onwards and this, coupled with increasing costs and local redevelopment, was seriously inhibiting the growth of the company's stage carriage services.

Maynes were extremely reluctant to adopt GMTs 15% fare increase in August 1980 and suggested that fares should be lowered in order to attract people away from their cars. The trial began during Easter 1981 and was accompanied by extensive advertising on buses and poster sites along Ashton New Road. Both GMT and Maynes cut fares by 50% throughout the day with a maximum off-peak fare of just 40p. The scheme would run for another nine or ten months, before being quietly abandoned in January 1982.

The introduction of this low fares experiment would also make a nonsense of the 'after' survey designed to measure the impact of the 346 on the company's takings. As a result, Maynes would never be recompensed for any abstraction made by the GMT service (although one could argue that the extension of the 209 more than made up for this).

Despite the recent extension to the 209 and its associated increase in revenues, operating costs such as fuel and crew wages continued to increase. Obviously something had to be done to stop this escalating further and, with the withdrawal of the last two Regents, the company was now prepared to introduce one-man operation. This was carried out on Tuesday 26th May 1981 when both the 209 and 213 were revised.

All buses now served Ancoats Hospital instead of Pollard Street and the 213 was diverted to operate in a revised loop around the Sunnyside Road estate. The company's buses had been serving Springfield Road since the early 'fifties. Now, however, the 213 was being altered to serve Chappell Road, Sunnyside Road and the full length of Greenside Lane. Service 209 (which had previously avoided

In December 1982, a former London Transport Fleetline arrived in Manchester to begin a new life in exile. DMS number 2163 (OJD163R) was pressed into service on a CIS contract and soon became a regular performer on the 209 and 213.

In 1985 two more former London Transport buses arrived. The first, OJD131R, was painted into this distinctive version of the Mayne livery which had all the hallmarks of its previous owner, Stevensons of Uttoxeter.

Sister vehicle OUC35R arrived in March 1985 after a brief spell with Mayne Group associate Barry Cooper Coaches. New to London Transport she came via Happy Days of Woodseaves.

In 1983 a Leyland Olympian double-decker was loaned to Maynes for evaluation. Registered A33MRN, its operating service was restricted to the Sunnyside Road route. The bus is now with Preston Borough Transport.

Coaches continued to be used occasionally on the bus routes. SND353X is a Leyland Tiger with Plaxton Supreme Express VI coachwork. On this occasion it was being used to replace one of Bristol VRs, which had been sent for a repaint in May of 1986. The Mayne Group fleet name has been removed from its sides in the expectation that it would receive route branding for the new Barnsley express service.

the estate by serving just Chappell Road) now operated the opposite way round to the 213, serving Greenside Lane and Sunnyside Road.

Things that could have been

Ashton New Road, once lined with shops and terraced houses from Manchester to Droylsden, was now dotted with large stretches of derelict land. The redevelopment of the area had led to a great many people being relocated to high rise blocks of flats or new housing estates such as those being constructed in Beswick and Clayton.

The company had been watching the development of the Beswick estate for some time now and in a meeting with GMT in June 1984, tabled a proposal for a new service linking the estate with both Manchester and Droylsden. The proposed all-day Monday to Saturday service would operate every hour and terminate at Ashton Hill Lane/ Gorseyfields, just beyond Market Street in Droylsden. Representatives from GMT agreed to consider the proposal, which would feature a similar financial arrangement to that on the 209/213, but indicated they were about to introduce their own service, numbered 189.

A further proposal put forward by the representatives from Maynes was a plan to reactivate the old X19 Manchester to Barnsley service. The luxury coach service would have operated on a limited stop basis between Manchester, Ashton, Stalybridge and Greenfield, and observe all stops from there to Holmfirth and Barnsley. Operating at a frequency of less than every two hours, full picking up and setting down rights in Greater Manchester were sought. The GMT representatives agreed to consider their reaction, but indicated that it was unlikely to be favourable without a suitably protective minimum fare at the Manchester end. They also commented on the apparently speculative nature of the proposal, with its likely lack of passenger generation. Were the picking up points on Ashton Old Road incidental they asked, or purely intentional?

The semi deregulated period

Since 1930, Road Service Licences had given operators a virtual monopoly on the route they were licensed to provide and independent bus operators were a rare thing in Britain's major cities. The Conservative Government had not been in power long when it set about privatising the nationalised industries. Mr Nicholas Ridley, MP and Minister for Transport, instigated a Government White Paper on the reorganisation and restructuring of the bus and coach industry. The deregulation of buses was heralded as a passengers' charter, which would free them from the monopoly of a regulated system and allow more room for competition, better services and lower fares. From the critics there were mainly cries of alarm and despondency.

To Maynes it represented a return to its roots, as it was about to go full circle and re-enter the deregulated world. Under the provisions of the Transport Act 1985 the need for bus services to have Road Service Licences was to be substituted with a Service Registration document. Any licenced operator could then register a bus service, subject to a system of quite stringent regulations.

Further provision allowed for the disposal of the National Bus Company and the Scottish Bus Group by privatisation. Public Transport Companies would be created in the major cities. Owned at 'arms length' by their Passenger Transport Authority, they would have to trade in a commercial environment without financial support, other than subsidies for services which they might gain by competitive tender.

Maynes began to look at its two services and try to determine how it might succeed in the post deregulation era. From deregulation day on the 26th October 1986, everything would change. All artificial operating boundaries would be removed and all protective agreements of the past would be declared null and void. Greater Manchester Transport would become Greater Manchester Buses Limited. Maynes would no longer be co-operating with an associate and be protected by an operating agreement. From then on they would be competitors.

The High Peak Pacers

With the former London buses in service, the first of the S-registration Bristol VRs was sent for a re-paint. VJA667S reappeared in a striking new variation of the company's livery, with a prominent 'M' flash between decks. The rear of the vehicle promoted a new venture by the company, 'Glossop to Manchester – the M Way'.

VJA667S is seen on the M67 Motorway on the first day of High Peak Pacer service 228.

The High Peak Pacers, as the routes were known, offered a new, fast and economical way to travel between the Glossop area of the High Peak and Central Manchester. Express services 228 and 229 were launched on 14th April 1986, operating every hour off-peak along the M67 motorway, with a more extensive service on Saturdays.

Services 228 and 229 commenced at the Royal Oak in Glossop, the 228 served Dinting, Hadfield, Padfield, Tintwistle and Hollingworth whilst the 229 served Simmondley, Charlesworth and Broadbottom. In Manchester the services stopped at Reddish Bridge, Belle Vue, Ardwick Green and Piccadilly.

Whilst Clippercards, Saver Seven tickets and concessionary fares were not available on the services, the company hoped it would be successful in convincing the Passenger Transport Authority that this would be in the public's interest. In the meantime, however, a period return fare was offered between Glossop and Manchester at £1 return.

Also launched from the same date was a new off-peak shoppers' bus between Henry Square in Ashton and Werneth Road in Simmondley. Service 238 operated approximately every two hours via Stalybridge, Mottram Rise, Hollingworth and Gamesley.

Left: MRJ8W was travelling the Mayne way from Glossop to Manchester on Monday 14th April 1986.

Lower left: Three of the coaches (numbered 52, 53 and 58) would become regular performers on the company's bus routes after deregulation. Leopard number 58 (MRJ358W) is putting in some practice on service 238 in Mottram.

Opposite page:

Top left: VJA667S operating on the non-stop peak hour express service 231. The bus has just dropped the last of its passengers on the Sunnyside Road estate and is heading back (out of service) to Manchester Piccadilly. Note the fleet number next to the nearside indicator lights.

Top right: Mayne number 16 at the junction of Medlock Street.

Centre left: Number 14 is seen in Littlemoss on service 234 (Micklehurst-Manchester).

Centre right: LRJ211P sits at Hazelhurst, the original terminus of service 233.

Foot: Number 13 sits in the shade at Uppermill on the short-lived Sunday service 235.

Service 231-235

The long-established services 209 and 213 were to be replaced by new services 231 to 235 which were launched on Monday 16th June 1986. Service 231 provided a peak hour 'non-stop' link between Manchester and Littlemoss, reverting to a normal stopping service on Sundays. New daily service 232 was basically an extension of the 209 from Hartshead to Oldham via Roundthorn. Despite objections by Oldham MBC over claims of traffic congestion, the route was approved by the Traffic Commissioners.

Services 233 and 234 also operated along the former 209 route as far as Waterloo. From there the 233 served Smallshaw and Hazelhurst,

whilst the 234 covered Top and Bottom Mossley and the village of Micklehurst. On Sundays the 234 became a 235, following the same route from Manchester to Top Mossley, but continuing to Uppermill for attractions such as the Alexandra Craft Centre, Saddleworth Museum and the Clough Bottom Garden Centre.

The Manchester terminus for each service became Piccadilly Bus Station, instead of the company's old terminus in Stevenson Square. Maynes, now actively promoting itself as 'a family concern', agreed with GMT to continue accepting concessionary fares, Clippercards and Saver tickets in exchange for continuing the 85/15% arrangement up to deregulation.

Chapter Six
Mayne's Big Cats and Small Merc

Bedfords continued to find favour with Maynes until the end of the 'seventies, when a change of policy led to a decision to purchase the heavy-weight Leyland Leopard chassis with the more powerful Leyland 680 engine. Like the Bedford VAM, the Leopard is noisy in performance but extremely economical in operation. Twelve examples, consisting of nine 12m (39ft long) models and three 11m (36ft long) models would be delivered between 1980 and 1982.

The first two, HDB354/5V, were fitted with 6-speed ZF synchromesh gearboxes (all subsequent deliveries were semi-automatics) and carried the very latest Plaxton Supreme IV coachwork. Moves were now being made towards a standardisation of livery, with a relatively uniform layout of lettering and fleetname styles. A policy of registering new coaches with 'invisible' fleet numbers in the 300s was also maintained, having started in 1978 with YNF347T.

The traditional red and cream livery was now applied in a much more modern manner based on Plaxton's own livery designs. The old-style trading name was replaced with the more bolder and singular 'MAYNE' title with the trading name 'Mayne of Manchester' emblazoned on the rear. Early attempts at marketing the family product had resulted in the slogan 'Travel the Mayne way'. This had been carried on the sides of the 1978 Bedfords with little noticeable effect. When they were later applied to two new Leyland Tigers, however, you could hardly fail to miss them.

Shortly before deliveries of the Leopards were complete, a thirteenth example was re-built at Ashton New Road from an early 1970 (ex Midland Red) chassis. This notable achievement by the engineering staff was later delivered to Plaxtons at Scarborough where it received a brand new Supreme IV body having been re-registered SNC366X.

The Tigers

The Leyland Tiger was launched in 1982 as the successor to the popular Leopard chassis. Like its counterpart, it was available in three lengths, 10m (33ft), 11m (36ft) or 12m (39ft), and fitted with air suspension to help counter competition from Volvo. Initially powered by the Leyland TL11 engine, the Tiger was later available with the trusty Gardner or popular Cummins L10 engine.

SND352/3X, delivered in March 1982, were 11m long examples fitted with Plaxton Supreme VI coachwork designed primarily for long-distance express work. Fitted with 53 seats, the vehicles were later re-configured to accommodate tables with transverse seating. They were also regular performers on the company's local bus services, especially after deregulation in 1986.

Maynes had now taken delivery of fifteen new coaches based on the heavier Leyland chassis over a period of two years and when the order was completed in July of 1982 only a handful of Bedfords remained. Most were to be replaced over the next two seasons with four Leyland Tigers with Plaxton's new high-floor Paramount 3500 coachwork. The last of the Bedfords to go were the 41 seaters (YNF350/1T) which, rather ironically, were replaced by yet another Bedford. A351KBA was a VAS5 and had a similar chassis layout to the erstwhile SB. Fitted with a 29-seat Plaxton Supreme IV body, this little coach was a midibus even before the term was first coined.

During those two seasons, the company invested around £700,000 in new coaches, giving it one of the most modern fleets in the area. The order for four Tigers and one Bedford was mirrored by a similar order for the family's latest transport concern – Barry Cooper Coaches.

Barry Cooper Coaches

Arnold Barrie Cooper, of 1 Mason Street, Howley, Warrington, acquired his first coach (a Burlingham-bodied Ford) in October 1963. Mr Cooper, a grocer by trade, used the 41-seater on private hire and contract work until a new Duple-bodied Ford was purchased in the spring of 1964. A succession of Bedfords and Fords then followed and by 1971, Coopers of Warrington had moved to their present headquarters at 110 Grappenhall Road, Stockton Heath. Mr Cooper now had a fleet of 10 coaches, which would soon be joined by an East Lancs-bodied AEC Regent V.

In common with other vehicles in the fleet, the Regent would not stay for long, being replaced in 1972 by a Leyland PD1 from Gateshead & District. Three years later in 1975, the firm acquired its first Leyland Leopard coach from Harris of Cambridge and purchased a brand new Plaxton-bodied AEC Reliance. Like Maynes, Coopers now began to standardise their fleet on heavy-weight coaches, gradually withdrawing the remaining Bedfords.

Mr Cooper's business empire was now beginning to crumble and towards the end of 1981 he approached Stephen Mayne with a view to selling him the assets of his coaching operation. After due consideration, the sale was agreed, and in January 1982, a new limited liability company – Barry Cooper Coaches Ltd – was established.

The sale had included a fleet of 20 coaches along with the licences, contracts, associated goodwill and the operating centre at Grappenhall Road. The shareholders of the new company were members of the Mayne family, but Barry Cooper Coaches was not a subsidiary of A. Mayne & Son Ltd.

There were gains to be made, however, through using Maynes' established reputation as a prestigious coach operator, and to take advantage of this, the trading name The Mayne Group was introduced alongside the company's local identity. Further gains were made through the adoption of Maynes' red and cream livery which not only replaced that of Coopers uninspiring white and black colour scheme, but enabled greater flexibility in fleet management and the ability to interchange vehicles between the two fleets if required.

The Barry Cooper fleet consisted of seventeen Leyland Leopards (two of which were early L2 models) and three Volvo B-58s. After a full evaluation it was decided that five of the Leopards and all three Volvos would be retired over the course of the next two seasons and Maynes' order for new Leyland Tigers was increased to accommodate the needs of the new associate company.

The last new vehicle delivered to Coopers had been a Plaxton Supreme-bodied Leyland Leopard delivered in March 1981. This had been registered ODJ417W and, in line with Maynes' policy of

Stephen Mayne stands proudly aloft the chassis of SNC366X before its despatch to Scarborough for fitment of its coachwork.

What the passengers never see – the intricacies of the modern chassis which keep the fitters busy with regular maintenance and safety checks.

The finished vehicle. SNC366X is seen in Blackpool shortly after entering service.

SNC363X was the last of the order for Leyland Leopards to be delivered and entered service in July 1982. The 57-seater has Plaxton Supreme IV coachwork.

This 12-seater minibus was acquired from O'Brien of Farnworth in August 1981 and mainly used alongside OJD163R on a private contract for the Co-Operative Insurance Society. It was sold to Vales Coaches of Manchester in April 1987.

The last Bedford acquired by Maynes was A351KBA, which entered service in April 1984. It was transferred to Barry Cooper Coaches in November 1990, staying in that fleet until March 1993.

Mayne Tiger Turbo. A370HNC has Plaxton Paramount 3500 coachwork.

registering new coaches with invisible fleet numbers, the five Tigers and one Bedford delivered in 1983/4 would contain the numbers 418-23 in their registrations.

Deregulation of Coach Services

The Transport Act of 1980 began the process of de-regulation with the abolition of the need for licences on long distance coach services. Services which set down their first passengers outside a radius of 15 miles were now exempt from the licensing system and free to devise their own fares and schedules. To Maynes, this meant they could now charge fares in accordance with the market, making the operation of excursions and tours that much more flexible.

In 1986, Maynes launched an 'improvement service programme' designed to bring the company's express, excursions and extended day tours completely up-to-date. The traditional holiday express services to Blackpool, Rhyl, Scarborough and York were supplemented with 15 new destinations, including a new Lincolnshire coast express for Cleethorpes and Skegness. Additional agents were also appointed in Greater Manchester (3), North Wales (4), Lancashire (2), Lincolnshire (6) and Yorkshire (2), whilst Maynes itself became a National Express agent.

Pick-up points in the area were extended to include Middleton, Glossop, Dinting Vale, Hadfield and Hollingworth and the excursions and tours programme was supplemented with tours to Scotland, South Wales, southern England and for the first time, to the Continent and Eire. The high-specification Tigers were put to use on extended day tours (marketed under the 'Super-Luxe' name) and in the late season, they operated the short continental tours to Boulogne and Amsterdam.

With rising unemployment in the area, 1985 prices were held on all excursions and holiday express services to attract the budget-conscious. Also new for 1986, was the Multi-Tour, which offered passengers a wider and better choice of tour itinerary including a wet-weather venue. Credit card bookings were also advertised by the company for the first time.

Attempts were also made to take over the London to Manchester service operated by Len Wright Travel and plans to introduce a Manchester to Barnsley and Oldham to Liverpool coach service were actively pursued by Peter Townley, the company's new general manager. This sudden surge of activity from a company which prided itself on its stability and a reluctance to change presented a confusing picture which was viewed uneasily by its managing director and employees alike. This conflict of opinions would eventually force a change of management and a return to traditional practices.

Mayne Group coaches from 1985

Four more Leyland Tigers were delivered in 1985, this time with Plaxton Paramount 3200II coachwork. The vehicles adopted 'real' fleet numbers for the first time since a short-lived attempt in 1959. Numbers 24 and 25 (B424/5RNA) went to Barry Cooper Coaches, whilst 49 and 50 (B349/50RNA) – which were fitted with Gardner engines – joined the Mayne fleet.

Vehicles exchanges between the two associated Mayne Group companies soon became a regular occurrence, as would the re-registration of coaches with private registrations. The first to find its way to Stockton Heath would be a former Kettlewell Leyland Leopard (PTO350R), acquired in 1982. This would be followed between 1985 and 1987 by the four Leopards purchased new in 1980 (HDB354-7V).

New coach deliveries in 1986 were three more Gardner-engined Leyland Tigers, this time fitted with high-floor, Plaxton Paramount 3500II coachwork. C426YBA joined the Barry Cooper fleet, whilst

Two Gardner-engined Tigers were delivered in 1985. 403BGO was originally B350RNA and is fitted with Plaxton Paramount 3200II coachwork.

C347/8YBA helped spearhead Maynes' improved excursions and tour programme. Their full-specification configuration featured 51 reclining seats, an on-board toilet, TV/Video system and drinks servery. The Mayne Group now had five such vehicles which it could call upon, although the separate entity of each company would mean that accounts and invoices would always be raised whenever any reciprocal help was given.

The Mayne Group had nineteen Leyland Tigers in its fleet in 1986 and around twenty-five Leyland Leopards, purchased both new and second-hand. There were also two short-wheelbase Bedfords. Early problems encountered with the Tigers included oil leaks and axle problems, all of which were soon rectified in the workshops. The two examples fitted with hydracyclic gearboxes also suffered from poor fuel consumption which led to the decision to sell these at an early stage.

Lymmville Coaches

The all-Bedford fleet of Lymmville Coaches of Lymm, Cheshire was acquired by Barry Cooper Coaches in the Spring of 1988. The acquisition included the contracts, vehicles and goodwill of the twenty year old company, but not the operating base in Garrasley Lane, Lymm. All five drivers and their Duple Dominant-bodied Bedfords were transferred to Stockton Heath.

The change back to Duple

The first vehicle to travel from Barry Cooper Coaches to take up residence with Maynes was a thirteen year old Leyland Leopard which arrived towards the end of 1986 having been rebodied by Duple. The company's allegiance had now returned to the Blackpool-based manufacturer, after an absence of some 24 years.

Price is often a considerable factor when deciding the choice of coachwork for new vehicle purchases and this, coupled with the fact that some of the Plaxton-bodied coaches in the fleet had been suffering from a mild form of corrosion, had made Duple the best option.

In January 1989, the Mayne Group took delivery of its first new coaches in three years. Barry Cooper received F27HNC, a Duple 320-bodied DAF, whilst Maynes took delivery of two Cummins-engined Leyland Tigers. F55HNC was fitted with a manual gearbox and a high-floor Duple 340 body, whilst F56HNC had a fully automatic gearbox and the lower Duple 320 body.

Maynes now had a coach fleet of 21 vehicles and in June 1989 acquired two more Leyland TL11-engined Tigers. Both came from Midland Red South and had Duple 340 bodies, configured for National Express work. C518WBF was traded in two months later, whilst C520WBF was transferred to Barry Cooper, where it would stay until 1994.

Bovas, DAFs and Javelins

Two Duple Dominant-bodied Leyland Leopards (GRF267V/ UWY62X) and two of the ex Lymmville Bedfords were traded in part-exchange for two new Bova Futura touring coaches in July 1990. The powerful and radically-styled Futuras are fitted with DAF 11.6 litre engines, ZF gearboxes and air suspension as standard. Designed to be more aerodynamic, with gently bowed sides, a raked back windscreen and a bulbous front-end, the coaches were painted in two eye catching liveries, one principally cream, the other mainly red.

Following the takeover of Leyland by Volvo and the discontinuation of the Tiger chassis, the next order for new coaches was placed with Dennis Specialist Vehicles. The Guildford-based manufacturer, perhaps by then better known for its fire engines and dust carts, launched its Javelin coach chassis in 1987. This thoroughly-engineered chassis went into full production in 1988 and is available in an 8.5m, 10m, 11m or 12m mid-engined format with Cummins C-series engines, ZF manual or automatic transmission and with the option of air or steel suspension.

The Mayne Group ordered four, two for the Mayne fleet and two for Barry Cooper. The first to be delivered in March 1991 was H51DVR, an 8.5m model bought to replace the very last Bedford in the Maynes fleet. Its short Duple 320 body can carry 37 passengers, compared to the Bedford's 29. Next to arrive was H52FDB, which also joined the Mayne fleet and was later followed by H28FVM and J29LJA, which were delivered to Barry Cooper. All three are 11m examples fitted with Duple 320 coachwork.

Two Duple 340-bodied Leyland Tigers were acquired from Midland Red South in 1989. One was later sold in part-exchange for new Scania buses, whilst C520WBF was transferred to Barry Cooper where it became FIL9386. It too was part-exchanged for new Scanias in 1994.

Both of Maynes Javelins appeared in an episode of Coronation Street in 1994. Outside shots were taken of the short wheelbase coach (H51DVR) with inside shots filmed on the 11m model. This enabled the camera and sound crews to get all of their equipment inside.

This wasn't the first time a Maynes vehicle has appeared on television, as the company had a starring role in the Channel 4 comedy 'GBH'. The appearance on Coronation Street was, however, their biggest appearance to date. Millions of viewers up and down the country, indeed throughout the world, no doubt appreciated them immensely for leaving one of the main characters – Derek Wilton – at a service station!

No new coaches have been purchased by the group since 1991, as the emphasis has now been placed on buying new buses for the Mayne fleet. Demonstration vehicles have appeared from time-to-time (usually when the company requires additional coaches at a time of peak demand). These have included a former Wallace Arnold Volvo B10M and a former Shearings Scania. As we go to press in August 1995 orders are about to be placed for new coaches, to be delivered late in 1995.

Of the existing fleet, the Leyland Leopards have recently been refurbished and repainted and the company hopes to get another five years service out of them. A further 24 Leopards were purchased in 1994, with most being immediately sold on to other operators or scrapped for spares. Plans to re-body two of these vehicles with East Lancs EL2000 bodywork have been superseded by the purchase of new single-decker buses. KVO146W has since been stripped of its old bodywork and placed in storage. Four Leopards, acquired in 1988 and 1990 have already been re-bodied for bus work and the company feels the more advanced Tiger chassis could eventually become a

Above: H51DVR, the famous 'extra' seen in an episode of *Coronation Street*, is a Duple 320-bodied Dennis Javelin.

Below: Bova Futura G57SBA seen in 1992 at the Disneyland theme park near Paris. Its sister vehicle is now the company flagship.

better candidate.

Meanwhile the Mayne Group's remaining Tigers are returning between 8 and 12mpg, with the Cummins-engined variants returning between 11 and 12mpg. A further Duple 340-bodied Tiger was purchased at an auction in September 1991. The former Highland Scottish vehicle was fitted with a Leyland engine and had a hydracyclic gearbox. It was sold in part exchange for new Scania buses in 1994. The trusty Gardner-engined models still remain, however, and one such vehicle has passed 500,000 miles without the need of attention. Maynes' coaches may be getting older, but they're as reliable as ever.

The British & Continental Tours

The ambitious improvement programme of 1986 failed to catch on and the following season featured a scaled-down programme of events. The holiday express service now only operated to the traditional destinations such as the Lancashire, North Wales and Yorkshire coasts. All the agency arrangements outside Greater Manchester were abandoned along with the company's status as a National Express agent. Out of the additional pick-up points introduced in 1986, only Hollingworth was retained as a regular departure point with Glossop only available on the holiday express services. One-off, eight day tours were gradually developed during the late 'eighties with more and more tours introduced to the Continent. Belgian and French hop-overs continued to prove popular as did the company's Christmas and New Year breaks.

In 1991, Maynes finally introduced an extensive European and British tour programme. Whilst it was accepted that the company couldn't compete with the major coach operators such as Shearings and Wallace Arnold, it was however able to offer similar holidays on a much smaller scale with the added incentives of free holiday insurance and a local departure point. Not for nothing does the company emphasise the advantages of using a local operator which guarantees that its holiday-makers will be on their way 'within an hour or less with no extra transfers'.

Brand new Bova Futura touring coaches equipped to the latest and highest standards were purchased in 1990 to operate most of the Continental breaks. An experienced team of drivers and couriers are provided throughout each tour and group bookings with tailor-made

itineraries are actively pursued. A good selection of additional pick-up points was also chosen for the new programme and included Altrincham, Sale, Stretford, Manchester, Salford, Eccles, Swinton, Irlams o'th Height, Rochdale, Oldham and Warrington. Reservations are handled centrally, eliminating the need for expensive agency commissions.

The 1991 programme proved to be very successful and in the following year, the company broadened its horizons with additional tours to Ireland, Scotland and the new EuroDisney theme park near Paris. The most popular tours now operate two or three times each year, whilst careful research ensures that Maynes continue to meet all of their customers needs.

Today, Maynes operate their traditional express coach services alongside an extensive excursions and tours programme to destinations throughout the country. Regular continental coach holidays now take in Paris, Amsterdam, Dublin, Denmark, Switzerland and the French Champagne area with feeder services serving 27 locations throughout Greater Manchester.

The company has also made a conspicuous success of selling air holidays to Jersey with return transfers from local pick-ups to Manchester Airport and the services of local representatives on the island. Clients can now choose from three different hotels and, during 1995, there will be no less than twenty-nine separate departure dates. A highly successful Christmas and New Year programme now operates each year to a wide selection of destinations which include Edinburgh, Jersey and of course Blackpool – the place where the Mayne coach holidays first began.

Now, some seventy-five years later, the company continues to pride itself in the services it provides and considers each and every one of its customers a friend. As a result, every year thousands of holiday-makers enjoy a satisfying holiday when they travel the Mayne way.

This line-up of Mayne Group coaches was taken one Bank Holiday at the Alton Towers theme park. With the exception of the Duple Laser (YUC765), all these Leyland Leopards have Plaxton Supreme coachwork.

Chapter Seven
Deregulation

Deregulation finally dawned on Sunday 26th October 1986, a relatively quiet day which, for most operators, was merely the lull before the storm. Britain's bus industry was about to undergo its biggest upheaval in fifty years, an upheaval that would see the emergence of new operators to challenge the old, and the gradual replacement of a state-owned monopoly with that of a private one.

Not all the services presently operated by GMT would be transferred to the new GM Buses limited company. Some routes, which were considered to be inviable without any form of financial support, were put out to tender by the Passenger Transport Executive. Interested operators could then bid for the contracts by stating the minimum subsidy that they would require to operate the service based on the assumption that they would keep all the revenue.

Maynes successfully tendered for new services 171, 172 and 175. The first two were replacements for the old 168 and 171 (Chorlton to Newton Heath) routes. Service 171 operated between Belle Vue, Gorton, Droylsden and Newton Heath, with the 172 continuing through Failsworth, Hollinwood and Oldham to the village of Higginshaw. Service 175 also served Higginshaw, Oldham and Failsworth and continued due south from there to the village of Woodhouses, replacing the 415 on the main Higginshaw Road and service 159 between Failsworth and Woodhouses.

These new routes took Maynes' buses into districts which for many years had represented the very core of the company's excursion and tour activities, and – perhaps rather ironically – would be operated with the aid of three Plaxton Supreme-bodied coaches until additional vehicles were purchased in 1987.

Yorkshire 'Puddings'

Maynes were no stranger to using dual-purpose coaches on bus work. Throughout the mid to late 'seventies, AEC Reliances were used extensively on the 213, usually on evening and Sunday duties. Even before then, it was not uncommon to see a coach performing stage carriage work along Ashton New Road. The operation of single-decker buses was however different. Indeed the last single-decker bus to be acquired by Maynes was back in 1945, when a Bedford OB had been purchased. Prior to that, less than a dozen or so examples had been operated.

When the company decided to replace the coaches on the tendered bus work, their gaze turned to West Yorkshire PTE and its stock of redundant single-deckers. In March 1987, five Leyland Leopards with Plaxton Derwent bodies were brought to Clayton. Nicknamed 'Yorkshire Puddings' by the staff, the 43 and 45 seat vehicles were restricted to marginal work with lower passenger loadings and allocated fleet numbers 2, 4, 6, 7 and 19.

The Mayne Group acquired a batch of nine Leopard service buses from West Yorkshire PTE in March 1987. UJX918M was one of five which joined the Mayne fleet. It is seen on Chappell Road in Droylsden operating peak hour service 231.

SCP342L was initially allocated to the Mayne fleet and is seen painted up in yet another version of the company's livery. The Plaxton Derwent-bodied Leopard would be sent to Barry Cooper in October 1987 in exchange for GWY691N.

Problems of a new era

Maynes had been 'testing the water' during the semi-deregulated period with the extension of the Droylsden and Hartshead routes. Services 231-5 provided the Oldham and Tameside area with new links with Manchester and these were consolidated into the new network at deregulation. The daytime services were becoming very popular, especially in the hillside town of Mossley. Service 234 which served the town en-route to nearby Micklehurst, was extended south, along the main Huddersfield Road, to the village of Carrbrook. The ambitious Sunday network was found to be inviable, however, and was reduced at deregulation to an hourly service 231 between Littlemoss, Droylsden and Manchester. This stretch of route had historically built up an enormous amount of customer loyalty and would remain the mainstay of the company's commercial operation.

The new network had its fair share of problems however, as the enormous popularity of the daytime routes often meant full buses passing stops in the Droylsden area (a fact not helped by the peak hour 231 which operated non-stop to and from Littlemoss). Another simmering source of complaints was the shoppers service 238 which quietly worked its way from Ashton to Simmondley. Many of the local residents were quite aghast at the sight (and sound) of the firm's Leopard coaches running past the end of their drive-ways. With its terminal point well away from the main shopping centre in Ashton and the lack of concessionary fares on the empty High Peak Pacers, these three routes were seemingly doomed from the start.

The family concern was well aware of the teething problems they were experiencing and promised to sort them all out as soon as possible. The High Peak Pacers and shoppers service 238 were withdrawn on 14th March 1987. One month later, the 231 was revised to observe all stops and extended along Newmarket Road to Waterloo, Green Lane. And so began the gradual redevelopment of the company's core network of routes, which would remain as popular as ever, generating a new loyalty amongst its regular passengers which is as strong today as it was in the days of Pioneer.

Maynes now had seventeen buses in their fleet with additional assistance coming from the three dual-purpose coaches when required. Further tendered bus workings continued to be added to the company's portfolio of routes, taking Mayne buses into Trafford Park and South Manchester (on services 290-4). Whilst this meant that the company was quite active during the week, it was a different story on Sundays,

as only one bus was required to operate the hourly 231 to Littlemoss.

Manchester's bus network was still in a state of flux however and the continued deregistration of commercial services by other companies would see the gradual increase in Maynes' Sunday workings as the year progressed. Having gained journeys on the 22 (Eccles to Stockport) and 394 (Stockport to Lane Ends), the company was presented with the opportunity of bidding for something a lot closer to home. GM had deregistered the Sunday service along Ashton New Road and the PTE promptly put the 216 and 236 out to tender. Maynes felt it could operate the services commercially and quickly stepped in to operate along routes which it had competed against for decades.

More Fleetlines

Prior to deregulation, Greater Manchester Transport had the largest bus fleet outside London, with around 2,500 vehicles. On Saturday 25th October, the needs of the newly formed Greater Manchester Buses Limited saw that fleet plummet overnight to an all time low of just over 1,700 buses. Around 600 of the redundant buses flooded onto the market and were later joined by older vehicles from the GM Buses fleet. The latter were sold through a joint sales venture with the dealership Kirkbys of Anston, near Sheffield. The purchase by Maynes of buses from their arch-rival would have seemed unthinkable just a few months before, but two Northern Counties-bodied Fleetlines were acquired from Kirkbys, swapping their orange livery for that of Maynes red and cream.

Expansion and confrontation

Following the loss of much of its daytime tendered work, the company began to look at expanding its commercial network. On Monday 18th January 1988, the company launched its new service 424 which operated from Ashton Bus Station, and along the main Oldham Road to an area known as Fitton Hill. From there, buses did a circuit of the estate before returning to Ashton. The two buses required to run the initial twenty minute service did so independently, even though the 424 crossed the path of the other Mayne bus services at Waterloo.

Five months later, the buses on the 424 began to inter-work with the rest of the network following the resurrection of an old SHMD route. Service 4 worked off the 233 at Carrbrook and ran via the village of Millbrook and the main Huddersfield Road to Stalybridge and Ashton. Buses could therefore work from one route to another,

The fleet number 18 is yet to be allocated to this former GMT Fleetline which is seen in Mossley on its first day in service in July 1987. The bright red livery seemed to suit the vehicles, making them much more attractive than their orange relations.

The end of the road is nigh for this Roe-bodied Fleetline. LRJ211P sits next to its replacement, a Northern Counties-bodied Fleetline acquired from Greater Manchester PTE.

This line-up of retired GM Fleetlines await new owners in 1987. WWH54L was subsequently acquired by Maynes and allocated the fleet number 21. It entered service in December 1988 and was withdrawn in March 1991 after the company acquired a batch of B20 Fleetlines from London Buses.

enabling greater flexibility and ease of crew changeovers which were carried out whenever buses passed the garage in Clayton.

The success of the new services and gradual increase in Maynes' operating area had not gone unnoticed. Up until now the company had been able to grow almost unhindered by its former associate, benefiting on most occasions by GM Buses attempts to cut costs and adapt to the new environment.

Manchester, in comparison with other UK cities, had seen a huge upsurge in competition at deregulation. At first it came from the local coach operators. Then United Transport launched its Bee Line minibus operation, posing an even greater threat to the former PTE company. By October 1987, there were 39 competing operators in the conurbation, a figure that would nearly double over the next five years.

GM Buses responded to the competition in various ways, buying a massive fleet of over 360 minibuses to see off the threat from Bee Line. This was completed in the summer of 1988 when the innovative minibus firm was sold to Ribble. Now GM Buses focused its attention on Maynes, and in a surprise move, registered four new services in direct competition with the growing family concern.

Starting on 15th August 1988, the occasional services ran three to four minutes in front of Maynes over the Manchester to Smallshaw, Hartshead, Mossley and Ashton to Mossley routes. By attacking the traditional Manchester to Droylsden routes, GM Buses was ending over twenty years of co-operation with the company. The first shots had been fired, yet within months GM had quietly withdrawn. They had made their point, however, and Maynes had been warned.

Buses to the Peak National Park

In May 1987, the company began operating a Derbyshire County Council contract to provide a summer Sunday and Bank Holiday service into the Peak National Park. The inaugural performance on the 395 was carried out by one of the coach seated Bristol VRs which left the conurbation by way of Belle Vue, Hyde and Glossop. From there, the VR would climb steeply over the Snake Pass and onwards, past the Derwent Dams, to the village of Castleton.

The following summer saw the 395 returning to Manchester by way of Buxton, New Mills, Hazel Grove and Stockport. This, in effect, created a grand circular service with a journey in the opposite direction (numbered 396) requiring another coach seated Bristol. A third would be required to operate the Pennine Rambler service 460. Departing Rochdale every summer Sunday, the 460 swiftly leaves Greater Manchester by way of Oldham, Ashton, Stalybridge and Glossop. The bus then climbs over the Snake Pass before winding through contrasting scenery and tiny High Peak villages to terminate at Matlock Bath. GMT initially operated this service in the summer of 1986, before it

passed to Rossendale. They, in turn, lost it to Maynes who have operated it ever since.

Fleet Renewal

Obtaining parts for certain vehicles in the fleet was becoming increasingly difficult, following the disappearance of Bristol, Daimler and Bedford. All but the latter had been swallowed up by the mighty Leyland concern, which would later become part of Volvo. One of the five Roe-bodied Fleetlines had already been scrapped for spares in 1987 and the company decided a year later to retire three of the remaining four.

To replace the Roe-bodied trio, five good quality middle-aged double-deckers were acquired from the redundant GMT fleet. Four

Below: Not many old Maynes buses manage to evade the scrapper's torch. LRJ213P, would return to the streets of Manchester under the ownership of Stuarts of Hyde, however, and was once again put to task on a service numbered 209.

Foot: A sight Arthur Mayne could only have dreamed of all those years ago. Fleetline number 4 (GND505N) stands proudly in Ashton Bus Station whilst operating service 216.

A Bristol VR in the snow. VJA667S is seen on the Fitton Hill estate operating service 424 to Ashton.

The resurrection of SHMD's service 4 occured on Monday 23rd May 1988. DMS number 5 is in Stalybridge, having been repainted into standard livery.

A sylvan scene in Glossop as one of the older VRs pauses en route to Castleton on service 395. The parking facility disappeared in the redevelopment of Glossop's Norfolk Square which saw this street pedestrianised.

entered service, whilst the fifth (BNE740N) was initially placed in storage at Maynes' new Fairclough Street coach depot. Six more would be purchased at various stages over the next year or so, half of which would be scrapped for spares. By the time BNE740N finally made it into service in the summer of 1989, the company had no fewer than ten ex GMT Fleetlines in service.

Mayne goes west

Whilst Maynes' operating area had retracted slightly at the end of 1987, the award of further GMPTE contracts in the last quarter of 1988 would see that operating area increase once more, as Maynes' buses began to serve the south and west of the city. Service 55 operated from Pendleton Precinct to Eccles Bus Station via Duchy Road and Irlams o'th' Height, crossing the East Lancashire Road more times than drivers cared to remember. The hourly Monday to Saturday service began on the 15th August 1988, and was usually operated by one of the single-deck buses in the fleet.

From the 25th September 1988 the dual-purpose coaches were again put to task on stage carriage work operating express service 500 between Bolton and Manchester Airport. Three were required to operate the hourly Monday to Friday daytime service. A month later,

from the 24th October, Maynes began operating works journeys into Trafford Park on services 54, 89, and 549. This was followed by Sunday workings on the 197 between Albert Square and Green End in South Manchester and weekend journeys on the 177 between Belle Vue and North Manchester General Hospital.

The Yorkshire 'puddings', now some 14 years old, were gradually replaced with more modern single-deckers commencing with the withdrawal of number 6 (UJX916M) in April 1988. There were still three left, however, when the company decided to buy three more Leyland Leopard buses, this time from Merthyr Tydfil Transport.

At the close of 1988 the bus fleet had grown to 23 vehicles, a steady increase from the deregulation fleet strength of 13 buses. The bus fleet had only just started to grow, but in the years to come it was set to grow even bigger.

Chapter Eight
Improving the Quality of Service

The average age of the bus fleet was now twelve years, with the oldest being an L-registered Fleetline, the newest two Bristol VRs acquired new in 1980. With six Leyland Leopard single-deck buses with bodywork by Plaxton and Willowbrook and nineteen double-deckers with bodywork mostly by Northern Counties, Maynes began to look at buying new vehicles once more.

After careful evaluation the company turned to Scania, the Swedish manufacturer which had been building buses for the British market since 1969, initially in a joint venture with Metro-Cammell Weymann. After severing its ties with the British manufacturer in 1980, Scania developed the N112, and the much cheaper K92 single-deck chassis. These, in turn, were developed into the much improved K93 and N113. The latter was now available in double-deck and single-deck form, although both models were promoted as environmentally responsible in terms of noise levels and exhaust emissions.

Maynes were impressed with the vehicle's simple construction and the ease with which it could be maintained. The company ordered two double-deck N113DRBs and chose bodywork by Northern Counties, as it was considered the best bodywork available. Also, by selling two coaches in part-exchange, the price was now both affordable and attractive at a cost of around £90,000 each.

The first vehicle was delivered in March 1989 and allocated the fleet number 12. Unfortunately, no sooner had F112HNC entered service than it was involved in a collision at the busy junction of Ashton New Road and Grey Mare Lane. A car which had jumped a red traffic signal caused extensive damage to the front and nearside corner of the bus, resulting in its hasty return to Wigan for repairs. The second vehicle, F113HNC, was delivered in May 1989. Fitted with semi-coach seating, it was soon a regular performer on the Pennine Rambler service 460 to Matlock Bath.

Despite a recent flurry of contract gains, Maynes' period of expansion had now come down a gear following the brief skirmish with GM Buses the previous summer. The core network of commercial services remained the 231-3 group of services to Littlemoss, Oldham and Carrbrook. Services 4 and 424 continued to rise in importance with a steady growth in passenger loyalty as they worked their way to and from Ashton. Elsewhere, one of the recently acquired Merthyr Tydfil Leopards could usually be found operating on the 55 route in Salford, whilst Maynes'w dual-purpose coaches performed on the 500 route to the airport. Other contracted work included works journeys to Trafford Park and a large amount of school and Sunday workings.

The first two Northern Counties bodied Scanias line up in Manchester's Piccadilly Bus Station one Sunday in May 1989.

Having spent much of 1988 in storage, BNE740N finally made it into service in the summer of 1989. New in 1976 it is a Northern Counties-bodied Fleetline.

Originally registered XJA566L, this former GMT Fleetline was acquired from the local grammar school operator, Hulme Hall Coaches, in whose livery it remained.

Fleetline number 14 at the Prestwich terminus of service 139.

Three Willowbrook-bodied Leyland Leopards were acquired from Merthyr Tydfil at the close of 1988. NTX361R entered service in November, whilst sister vehicles NTX362/3R entered service in the New Year. The bus is on Manor Road in Droylsden.

When GM reduced the frequency on its Bury New Road service to every hour, the PTE responded by putting out a tender for journeys on the opposite half hour. Maynes was the surprised winner of the contract and from 3rd April 1989, buses coming into Manchester on the 232 would operate one round trip on the 139 to Prestwich, before heading home on the 231 to Littlemoss.

One month later, the company gained the 357 route between Ashton, Audenshaw and Littlemoss. This hourly service, which ran past the former Maynes terminus at Kershaw Lane, was a GM Buses post-deregulation initiative. It was diverted via the Sunnyside Road estate and revised to terminate at Clockhouse Avenue from 25th September. From the same date, Maynes moved the terminus of its Manchester services to the Arndale Bus Station to make way for the new Metrolink station in Piccadilly and introduced a Sunday service on the 233 to Tameside Hospital.

Scanias and Warriors

The 1978 Bristol VRs were now unreliable and expensive machines to operate. With this in mind, the company decided to trade all three into a dealer (along with C518WBF) in September 1989 in part exchange for three more Northern Counties bodied Scanias. The first of their replacements (G115SBA) appeared at the Bus Show in Birmingham over the weekend of 21st/22nd October, before arriving in Clayton to enter service on the 1st November. G116SBA arrived in December and was followed in the new year by G117SBA.

The management at Maynes were still keen to update their small single-deck bus fleet, however, and a trip to Loughborough was made to consult with the Willowbrook engineering company. The firm's Warrior body was developed to appeal to operators requiring a low cost single-deck bus body, either on a new chassis or to re-body an older one. The availability of large numbers of well-engineered Leyland Leopards, capable of further mileage yet with unsuitable bodies had led to the Warrior body appearing on a number of chassis for various operators.

A few weeks after their visit, the company was presented with the opportunity of buying one of these vehicles which was being offered for sale by Perry of Bromyard. GDZ3841, was already painted in a livery similar to that used by the Mayne Group and, after selling one of the Barry Cooper Leopards in part-exchange, entered service with Maynes in February 1990.

Two months later, three more elderly Leyland Leopards were

Upper: Coaches were once again needed for stage carriage work in September 1988, after the company won the contract to operate the Monday to Friday daytime service on the 500 (Bolton to Manchester Airport). UWY62X was acquired from West Yorkshire in January 1989 and is seen in the paint shop prior to completion of its identity change.

Lower: Another Leyland Leopard was acquired from Merthyr Tydfil in November 1989. OWO234Y has a Duple Dominant bus body and is fitted with coach seats. It is seen in Eccles Bus Station in 1989, operating service 55 between Eccles and Pendleton.

acquired from Jowitt of Tankersley. Two were dispatched to Loughborough for re-bodying and re-registered LIW1322 and LIW1323 respectively. One of the Merthyr Tydfil machines (NTX362R) then followed, having already been re-registered NIB7625. All three had been given brand new bodywork for less than £100,000.

One of the stars of the 1989 Bus Show was G115SBA, seen here on Sunnyside Road.

Until the end of 1994, G117SBA carried commerative lettering marking 'Seventy Years of Friendly Service'.

GDZ3841 was acquired from Perry of Bromyard and is currently the only bus in the fleet to have been renumbered three times.

This 1973 Leyland Leopard was one of three acquired as chassis only in May 1990. One was scrapped for spares whilst the other two were rebodied at the end of the year to a design having some affinity to Leyland's Workington-built Lynx. LIW1323 is seen on Manor Road in Droylsden early in 1991.

Welsh Warrior. NIB7625 was previously NTX362R, one of the three Merthyr Tydfil Leopards acquired in 1988.

70 Years of Friendly Service

Unlike the preceding year, the company's seventieth anniversary in 1990 was marked by a period of carefully planned expansion. From the 11th November, the highly popular service 4 was extended from Ashton via Smallshaw and the usual Maynes route through Littlemoss to Manchester. Re-numbered 234, it introduced further new links for the people of Carrbrook, Millbrook and Stalybridge, who also gained an additional service (numbered 235) which boosted the frequency to every 30 minutes.

The 235 was in fact an extension of the company's 357 route which now operated between Manchester and Mossley via Clayton, Droylsden, Audenshaw, Ashton and Carrbrook.

The 424 was extended from Fitton Hill to Oldham and once again operated independently from the rest of the network. In Salford, service 55 was extended the short distance from Pendleton Precinct to Manchester Arndale, whilst the 139 was extended from Prestwich to Whitefield and Bury. Both of these services were now operating on a commercial basis without any form of subsidy from the PTE.

Contract gains during 1990 had seen Maynes operating between Manchester and the Salford Enterprise Zone on the short-lived 174/5 routes (they were withdrawn after just six months in November), whilst the award of a Sunday contract led to the company's buses running on the 57 route to Bank House (near Higher Blackley).

The family's red and cream buses could now be seen throughout North, South and East Manchester and the boroughs of Bury, Oldham, Salford, Tameside and Trafford. Their fleet of 21 double-deckers contained five new Scanias, whilst four out of the five single-deckers had new Warrior bodywork. Maynes was now moving forward with confidence and at the end of 1991 would attempt to acquire Shearings local bus operations in Bolton.

Opposite page:

Top: DMS number 1 at the Droylsden (Clockhouse Avenue) terminus of service 357.

Foot: The Pink Lady and last of the old guard. DMS number 3 was repainted in 1990 to carry this overall advertisement for GMPTEs *Every Bus Saver* ticket. OJD163R is now the only remaining member of the company's pre-deregulation bus fleet and is seen here at a Trans Lancs Historic Vehicle Rally in Heaton Park.

Old soldier LRJ210P looking rather splendid in this, its final livery. The bus was scrapped for spares in November 1990.

Chapter Nine
Fleetlines and Falcons

Deregulation was now nearly five years old, during which time bus fares had increased every year by around 10% and annual passenger journeys had fallen in Greater Manchester by some 100 million to an all time low of just 256 million. Many passengers did not fully comprehend what was going on in the deregulated bus industry, nor the economics behind the annual fare increases.

With as many as 70 different bus operators in the area, Maynes was suffering from increased competition, diluted revenues and increased costs, just like its former associate. There was still a large degree of rivalry between these two operators, especially on the Ashton New Road and Bury New Road corridors and this would eventually lead to another bitter confrontation.

On 21st April 1991, GM Buses extended its Ashton to Droylsden service through to Manchester. Service 382 had been formed at de regulation through the splitting of the old 346 route (Droylsden to Newton via Littlemoss, Ashton & Hyde). Maynes had already found itself in competition with the recently-formed Pennine Blue operation and was now coming under attack from GM as well.

From 7th May, the family concern pulled off the 55 route in Salford and transferred the vehicles to service 424. This was then diverted away from Oldham and extended via Limeside, Failsworth and Newton Heath into Manchester (Stevenson Square). Although it competed with GM's 76 route between Manchester and Newton Heath, for most parts it followed its own unique route, creating further new links for the local populace.

From the same date, the 139 route along Bury New Road gained a direct service to Bury, which avoided the usual detour around Carr Clough. Maynes' service 140 provided a fast alternative to GM Buses service 135 which operated via Bury Old Road and took 45 minutes to reach the town. The success of the new 140 and extended 424 would prompt GM Buses to copy the routes just over a year later.

Maynes' network of subsidised services also grew during 1991, following the loss of the Trafford Park and Airport services the year before. The evening service on the 188 route (Manchester to Chorlton) was gained from 25th March and was followed by the evening service on the 139 to Prestwich. Maynes then started serving Haughton Green, near Denton, gaining a Sunday journey on the 347 from Ashton. Next came the local 349 route which Maynes initially shared with Citibus during the week, followed by peak hour journeys on the 226 into Manchester. This, along with peak hour journeys into Trafford Park on the 54 was operated by the coach division.

The first Dennis Falcon joined the fleet in January 1991 and, in a marked change of policy, entered service in the yellow and dark grey livery of its previous owner Berks Bucks.

Right: This former Wilts & Dorset Fleetline was new to London Transport in 1976 and was acquired in November 1990. KUC969P, seen here in Ancoats, initially ran in serivce in NBC red and white until being repainted in the Spring of 1991. It was transferred to the Barry Cooper fleet in July 1994.

Below: The rear of the B20 version of the Daimler Fleetline showing the distinctive ducting which formed part of the means of reducing noise emission levels.

Fleetlines and Falcons

London DMS buses had featured in the fleet since 1983 and it was hardly surprising when the nation's capital retired its remaining Fleetlines, that Maynes would be a willing purchaser. Four were in the fleet already, with the latest vehicle (KUC969P) having been bought from Wilts & Dorset to replace the last of the Roe-bodied Fleetlines which was scrapped at the end of 1990.

Eight of the B20 quiet variants (identifiable by their tall ventilator chimneys at the rear) were brought to Clayton in March 1991. DMS number 2452 had unfortunately broken down on the way and was immediately returned and exchanged for THX303S (DMS2303). All the B20s had a dual door layout which was essential for operations in the busy capital, but not quite so necessary in Manchester. It was decided that seven B20s would have their centre doors removed and replaced by a fourth window bay. This would enable the company to increase the seating capacity to a more typical 75 seats, and when combined with their high standing capacity of 21 passengers, the B20s became the ideal replacement for some of the ex GMT Fleetlines. The remaining B20 (THX496S) would be cannibalised to provide the necessary parts, but not all vehicles could be converted immediately. As a result, THX322S and THX579S went into service on 11th March 1991 with their centre exits blocked off. Four more B20s would be acquired in February 1992, only one of which would enter service.

Dennis Specialist Vehicles launched its Falcon chassis in 1980 to take advantage of some municipal operators' desire to have a Gardner-engined single-decker. Maynes' first Falcon arrived in January 1991 from the Wycombe Bus Company. Wycombe's parent company, the Oxford Bus Company was on the lookout for more second-hand Bristol VRs and offered to swop the Falcon for MRJ8/9W, the last of Maynes' Bristols. The family concern had been looking to sell these two vehicles for some time and considered it to be a fair transaction. A101DPB had 49 coach seats inside, having been re-bodied in 1987 with Wadham Stringer's Vanguard bus body. It was the only one of its type delivered to the National Bus Company.

Chesterfield Transport had however taken nine examples in 1983/4. Four had bodywork by East Lancs with the remaining five fitted with Marshall's Camair-80 bodywork. Maynes were keen to buy more of these Gardner-engined workhorses and arranged to purchase the five Marshall-bodied examples. Delivered in November 1991, A44-8YWJ, were regular performers on the Altrincham Rail Replacement Services in the first quarter of 1992.

Return of the trams

Trams returned to the streets of Manchester in April 1992 after a 43 year absence. The new Metrolink trams were the latest light rapid transit units, capable of running on both rail and street track. Maynes had played an active part in providing replacement bus services for the Bury and Altrincham lines during their conversion

This Seddon Pennine was acquired in January 1991 for school contract work. The 53 seater is fitted with the dateless Alexander AYS body and was sold in 1993 to a bus operator in Rochdale who now trades as 'Pioneer'.

Despite the sudden influx of DMSs, most of the ex-GMT Fleetlines continued to soldier on. YNA328M had been acquired in 1988 and originally entered service as number 22. Now carrying the fleet number 8, the bus departs from Bury Interchange on service 140. Note the illegal spotlight arrangement.

There were four DMS class Fleetlines in the fleet when the company decided to purchase eight more from London Buses. These were of the B20 variant, and two imediately entered service in their London red. THX579S is in Piccadilly.

THX303S was the third B20 to enter service and the first to be painted into the standard livery. With a revised indicator display, taken off a scrapped Northern Counties Fleetline, the bus initially carried the fleet number 28. However, within days of entering service it would be re-numbered 33.

Number 34 also entered service in the company's livery, but carried no front destination equipment. The large destination apertures in the four older DMSs were hardly used and it was decided that a much neater layout could be built into their frontages which omitted the 'via' display. The B20s would be similarly converted once the necessary parts became available.

to Metrolink and the success of one of its routes inspired the family concern to try and compete with the tram once more.

Service 9 had been a Monday to Friday peak hour replacement for the suspended rail service to Altrincham, serving Oxford Road, Deansgate, Old Trafford, Stretford, Sale and Timperley. The closure lasted for about six months, during which time Maynes managed to build up a large amount of customer loyalty on the contra-flow service. Passenger perceptions around this period were very much anti-tram and so four of the busiest journeys were retained by the company on a commercial basis in the hope that passengers would remain loyal to the bus route. Within weeks of the trams being permitted to run through to Altrincham, however, most of the bus passengers had taken to using the new tram service and service 9 was abandoned less than two months later in August 1992.

On the Bury corridor, GM Buses had introduced express services based on some of the PTE's original rail replacement routes, but even this failed to compete effectively with the new Metrolink system. Further routes were added along Bury New Road dealing the eventual death blows to Maynes services 139 and 140.

Another battle begins

On 6th April 1992, GM Buses made further service cuts and closed its depots at Altrincham, Swinton, Rochdale and Tameside. Services in Tameside were divided up amongst the depots at Hyde Road and Oldham, and the remaining Ashton local services were discontinued. Maynes immediately stepped in to operate the 329 (to Hurst Cross) and 332 (to Hartshead) on a commercial basis, as GM Buses head-to-head competition with the company began to take a turn for the worse.

GM Buses journeys on the peak hour 186 route were extended to operate solely between Littlemoss and Manchester from 12th

A B20 with revised destination equipment heads into Manchester on the extended service 424. The success of both the revised 424 and new 140 would prompt GM Buses to copy routes just over a year later.

Having recently bought a dozen B20 Fleetlines from London Buses, the sudden appearence of a Leyland Titan at the end of 1992 was hardly surprising. After a period of evaluation, the company decided not to purchase any Titans on the grounds that they are extremely thirsty on fuel. With that, and at a costly 5 mpg, the bus travelled to Merseybus, never to be seen on Ashton New Road again.

Five Dennis Falcons were acquired from Chesterfield Transport in November 1991, taking up the fleet numbers 44 to 48. The bodywork is the very distinctive Marshall product.

For a period of six months Maynes ran a regular Monday to Saturday daytime service over GM Buses peak hour 186 route, extending it to operate over the former 357 (Droylsden - Audenshaw - Ashton) route to terminate at Tameside Hospital. This ex-Chesterfield Falcon is en-route to Manchester and is emerging from the Sunnyside Road estate shortly after the journeys were introduced in October 1992.

April. This peak period service now shadowed Maynes' traditional services through the Sunnyside Road estate and it would not be long before they adopted the service number 231. The remaining portion of the 382 to Ashton was amalgamated into the new midibus route between Chorlton and Tameside Hospital, which was numbered 168. The residents of the Sunnyside Road estate now had more buses to choose from than ever before.

To counter GM's latest moves Maynes revised all its services from 5th October 1992. This complicated set of changes started the company's gradual daytime withdrawal from Bury New Road and a gradual increase in its presence throughout Droylsden, Newton Heath and Failsworth. To keep up with all the changes, additional vehicles continued to be purchased with three ECW-bodied Leyland Fleetlines being added to the fleet at the end of the year, having come from Clydeside 2000.

Towards the end of 1991, Scania number 13 had this dark-blue advertisement painted on its rear, announcing the company's forthcoming coach tours to the new Euro Disney theme park in Paris.

Three ECW-bodied Leyland Fleetlines were acquired at the end of 1992 to meet the needs of the expanding network of local bus services. Two arrived in November and were followed a month later by ULS663T.

Chapter Ten
Darts and Dominators

The Dennis Lance is a highly competent city bus of simple construction. Introduced in 1992, Maynes expressed an early interest in the chassis, evaluating an Alexander-bodied demonstrator in May of that year. J110SPB gave a good performance, but it was felt that the price tag was too expensive and there was a considerable difference between that and the price of its smaller stablemate, the Dennis Dart.

Introduced at the Motor Show in 1988, the Dart has a lot of the advantages of a big bus. The rear engine, for instance, permits a wider entrance at the front and the layout allows a low step height. This, combined with low running costs, outstanding performance and great manoeuvrability, sealed its eventual success. The midibus is available in three lengths, (8.5m, 9m and 9.8m) and is fitted with a Cummins B-series 130bhp turbo-charged engine and an Allison gearbox mounted in-line at the rear.

Maynes ordered two 9.8m models in 1992 for use on a new PTE contract. The company had last run on the 171 route back in 1987. Since then the route had been operated by Yelloway, Burnley and Pendle, East Midland and latterly Bee Line. The service now operated between Newton Heath and Withington Hospital and the Dart's ingredients made it an ideal vehicle for the route. Fitted with a stainless steel-framed Marshall body,

the Darts can accommodate 40 seated passengers. K28XBA was delivered in November 1992, and was followed by K29XBA in January 1993.

The Dennis Dominator was launched in 1977 and found a ready market amongst the smaller municipal fleets, although the largest order came from South Yorkshire Transport. After experiencing one or two problems with the five Scanias, Maynes originally ordered two Dominators and one Scania for delivery in 1993. It was intended to send all three to Northern Counties, but problems over production dates meant that the Wigan-based manufacturer lost the order. Maynes went instead to East Lancs, a company which, many years ago, had built bodywork for some of the AEC Regents. A cancelled order by Strathclyde Buses meant that in the last week of February 1993, the family concern could take delivery of three Dennis Dominators, registered K36/7XNE and K38YVM. The trio were originally allocated the Strathclyde registrations K216-80GD and were fitted with transversely mounted Gardner engines. The Scania would follow soon after, allocated the registration L114DNA and the fleet number 14.

A newly-delivered Dennis Dominator double-decker poses alongside a five month old Dennis Dart in March 1993.

Consolidation

The British bus industry was by now embarking on a period of consolidation. The former National and Scottish Bus undertakings were in the hands of private owners and most of the former municipals had either been taken over or ceased trading altogether. Of the former PTE companies, Yorkshire Rider, Busways, West Midlands Travel, Merseybus and Strathclyde had all been privatised. South Yorkshire, which had now adopted the title Mainline, went in November 1993, leaving just GM Buses.

The Government in its infinite wisdom ordered that the company be split in two in order to promote competition – a word which slips easily off the tongue in Greater Manchester. On 19th December 1993, GM Buses was split into two separate companies in preparation for sale the following year.

A number of big bus-operating groups, such as Stagecoach, had now evolved to pick at the carcass of de-regulation, picking off the large independent and privatised concerns one by one. Two out of the top three already had a subsidiary in Manchester and the third would soon purchase PMT, Pennine Blue and Yorkshire Rider. Other large bus operating groups controlled Citibus and Finglands, a company which Maynes had considered purchasing, but now owned by East Yorkshire. Maynes itself has been approached by agencies acting on behalf of the big operating groups, but the company would resist the temptation and politely decline each offer.

Pastures new and old

GM Buses continued to de-register its loss-making services in a further attempt to cut costs and Maynes quietly followed in its wake, picking up some of the pieces. The daytime service on the 220 along Ashton Old Road was withdrawn in January 1993. Maynes immediately stepped in to operate the route commercially, adding the evening and Sunday service from 28th February. The evening contract on the 169 (Droylsden to Southern Cemetery) also came up for renewal at the same time and the company registered this commercially as well.

From 28th February 1993, new service 170 was introduced between Haughton Green, Belle Vue, and Withington Hospital. This replaced service 349 which Maynes had been operating in Haughton Green since September 1991. Operating every hour, the supported service requires the use of two buses and was extended in September 1993 to Cheadle. It was further extended to Cheadle Hulme less than a year later.

Back on the company's traditional patch, GM Buses had been steadily increasing the frequency on its competing 231 service, and had introduced a Saturday afternoon service from 5th December 1992. Maynes revised its services with effect from 18th April 1993, increasing its peak hour frequency between Manchester and Littlemoss to every 5 minutes. Between the two, the Sunnyside Road estate was becoming swamped with buses, leading to a string of complaints from concerned residents. It was not a situation of which the company could be proud, but this was traditionally Maynes' operating territory and had to be defended.

On the 30th January 1994, Maynes began to consolidate its bus network once again. The Ashton to Failsworth and Manchester services were re-hashed and the route through Audenshaw and Droylsden (Market Street) was withdrawn. Eight months later, Maynes would pull off the long-established 424 route, after its profits were chipped away at both ends by the competition, choosing to concentrate its efforts on the Droylsden and Mossley areas instead.

K29XBA was the second Dennis Dart to enter service with the company. It is seen in March 1993 shortly after the introduction of service 170.

The company had been operating service 332 (Ashton to Hartshead) since the closure of GM Buses Tameside depot. In October 1992 the route was extended via Oldham and Failsworth to Manchester. Six months after that, it was further extended from Ashton to Manchester via the 186 route, creating a large circular service, with journeys in the opposite direction numbered 336. K36XNE is operating on service 332 in Droylsden and just about to pull onto the main road, heading towards Ashton.

This East Lancs-bodied Dennis Dominator was originally intended for Strathclyde Buses and had been allocated the registration K217OGD.

Having returned to operate service 171, the company now found itself operating into Trafford Park again on services 290 to 292. The supported services now operate from Manchester, with the latter two only running in the Monday to Friday peak period. Service 290 on the other hand operates every day requiring two buses. The two Dennis Darts which entered service on 1st February 1994 (L26/7FNE) are regular performers on these services.

Apart from the South Manchester and Trafford Park services, much of the company's tendered service work now takes place on a Sunday. On this day, Maynes' buses can been seen throughout North, South and East Manchester, Tameside, Trafford, the High Peak and, during the summer months, as far away as the Peak National Park.

A new beginning

The two parts of GM Buses were sold to their employees in March 1994. Both are now very vulnerable to competition and takeover, with their respective managements realising at an early stage that it would be impossible to fight a bus war on all fronts. A cease fire has now been agreed between a number of concerns and on most corridors there exists what can only be described as a co-ordinated rivalry amongst operators.

GM Buses South continues to compete with Maynes for traffic on the Droylsden services and the family concern has responded by increasing its daytime frequencies and introducing yet another new service between Droylsden, Littlemoss, and Ashton. Using the same degree of foresight once used by Arthur Mayne, the company purchased two new Scania single-deckers at the close of 1994, specifically for use on the new service 167.

M42ONF and M113RNK are fitted with the Northern Counties Paladin bus body. Unlike other vehicles in the fleet, these 51 seaters are fitted with a 'kneeling' facility, making them more accessible to passengers who find boarding and alighting difficult. This small consideration makes life easier for the company's customers and is no doubt rewarded in kind, for it is customer loyalty that has been the biggest single factor in the company's success. It was what mattered to Arthur Mayne in 1920; the one ingredient that has steered it through every hardship, and one which Maynes continues to gather to this day.

In early 1929, Arthur Mayne bought the Pioneer bus operation and began to develop a reputation for a reliable and regular timetabled service, through punctuality, low fares, courteous staff and by investing in new vehicles. More than sixty years later, it is now Stephen Mayne who ensures that the company's reputation continues to go from strength to strength.

With two East Lancs-bodied Scania double-deckers delivered in January 1995, the Maynes bus fleet now comprises 23 double-deckers and 16 single-deckers. Of these 17 are less than six years old, making it one of the most modern bus fleets in Greater Manchester. Add to this the coach division with 20 vehicles and the fleet of Barry Cooper Coaches (with a further 23 vehicles) and you have an operating group which had a turnover of over £5.3 million in 1994.

The management at Maynes now feel that the company has reached its optimum size but does not rule out complementary acquisitions should the opportunity arise. Eventually, it is hoped that another generation of the Mayne family will join the company and so its future will ultimately lie in their hands. One thing is for certain, however, and that is the Mayne Group will continue to do what it does best as it quietly looks forward to its centenary, as a family concern.

Two more Dennis Darts were delivered at the end of January 1994. Both L26/7FNE carry the restyled Marshall Dartline body as seen here.

Maynes operate a large number of school bus services in the Manchester and Tameside areas. Here three different representatives from the fleet can be seen loading up at Droylsden High School.

Low-floor buses are the latest concept and a current industry 'buzzword'. Maynes evaluated this East Lancs-bodied Scania L113CRL in December 1994 before it had its centre exit removed and returned to Greater Manchester to do a further tour of interested operators.

Maynes' recent deliveries have included no less than four Scanias – two L113s with Northern Counties bodywork and two with bodywork by East Lancs. Note the 'Kneeling Bus' sign on the side of No. 43.

Chapter Eleven
Maynes in operation

Most passengers who travel the Mayne way will have given little thought as to what goes on behind the scenes to ensure their bus or coach turns up when they expect it, and that it will take them safely to their destination. To the casual observer Mayne's Garage is probably perceived as little more than a shed in which the company keeps its buses, but a properly run garage, staffed with expertly trained personnel is essential to the company's efficient and reliable operation.

Around 120 staff are currently employed by the company, consisting of 93 drivers, 9 engineers, 5 cleaners, plus 12 administrative and operational staff. Overseeing the entire operation is the company's general manager, Gradyn Thompson, who is also a director of the company. Other key personnel include Frank Yates, the company's coach operations manager, Alan Palmer, accounts controller and Alastair Nuttall, bus operations manager.

As mentioned in the previous chapter, there are currently 59 vehicles in the fleet, comprising 39 buses and 20 coaches. All the buses are based at Mayne's Garage on Ashton New Road and, since 1989, the coach division has had its own garage at Fairclough Street in Clayton. The company's workshop at Ashton New Road looks after the whole fleet however, and washing and refuelling of both buses and coaches is carried out there each day.

Things start very early at Ashton New Road during the week with the first driver reporting for duty at 04:45 to take out the 05:15 Manchester to Trafford Park journey on service 290. On Saturdays this journey does not operate and so the first driver will not report until 05:50, by which time the garage will have been open some twenty minutes. On Sundays Mayne's buses operate further afield and the garage is opened at 05:15, when the first driver arrives to take out the bus that will work the 06:15 Altrincham to Manchester journey on service 263.

Before taking out a bus, the driver has to report to a member of the operations staff in order to complete the sign-on procedure. Here, the driver will collect the appropriate running board and be given a computerised module for the Wayfarer ticket machine. He or she will also be allocated a vehicle.

The 'sign-on' procedure will be repeated by drivers throughout the day until the last driver reports for duty in the middle of the afternoon. In the event of a driver failing to report, then either the 'early garage driver' or 'late garage driver' will be used to cover the duty.

Maynes are fortunate in that most of their services run past the company's premises, simplifying crew changeovers. As a result most of the drivers' meal breaks can be taken at the garage. All vehicles in the fleet are fitted with two-way radios which are invaluable for ensuring safety of passengers and drivers and, in the event of a mechanical problem being reported, vehicle changeovers can also be accommodated with minimum disruption to services.

Vehicle allocation and engineering requirements

In July 1995, the company's peak vehicle requirement called for 33 buses during the week (reducing to 30 during school holidays), 28 on Saturdays and 25 on Sundays. Constraints will be placed on the allocator if the duty works on a journey subsidised by GMPTE, as the allocated vehicle will have to meet certain criteria. These may govern the vehicle's age and size, its step height and destination equipment, and even its internal specifications. The company currently has 29 vehicles which meet the PTE's requirements.

By the very nature of the subsidised services, with their lower passenger loadings, it is usual for single-deckers to operate them. There is, therefore, a fixed set of duties for sixteen single-deckers – one more than the company currently has available. From the 1st August 1995, however, one of the ex-Trent Willowbrook-bodied Leopards will be entering service and, at the time of writing, has just been taken out of storage and is being made ready by the engineers.

Each day the operations staff maintain a record of which vehicles are allocated to each duty and will have been made aware of which vehicles are due for servicing by the engineers. These vehicles are usually allocated to part-day workings and are serviced during the period they are not required. A driver-led defect reporting system also ensures that all faults are reported to the engineers and, if necessary, may warrant keeping the vehicle in for examination.

The engineering department will handle most requirements in-house, although it is common practice for vehicles to be sent to a third party for repainting or major repair work. All other tasks will be carried out in the company's workshop, which has accommodation for four vehicles with an inspection pit capable of handling two of these at any one time. Mobile vehicle lifts are also used and, in addition, will permit a fifth vehicle to be inspected on the forecourt, if required.

The team of nine mechanics and fitters work on the vehicles throughout the day, and sometimes into the night, ensuring that nothing goes unchecked. Buses undergo a safety check once every two weeks where all safety-related matters such as brakes and all interior and exterior lighting are tested. An even more thorough examination takes place every four weeks, when the monthly check is carried out. This detailed examination is similar to an MoT test and will cover everything in the safety check together with other items such as tyre pressure and battery condition; all vehicles are also serviced every 12,000 miles. Once any remedial work has been completed the vehicle will undergo a road test and, after being signed-off as satisfactory, will be re-allocated for duty.

On a typical Saturday at the end of July 1995, one of the double-deck Scanias had been despatched to West Pennine Trucks for maintenance and six other vehicles were due to receive attention in the company's own workshop at Ashton

New Road. These included Dennis Falcon A101DPB and Leyland Leopard GDZ3841, which were both in for electrical repairs. New single-deck Scania M113RNK was undergoing its MoT test, whilst one of the ex-Chesterfield Falcons was awaiting preparation. There were also two other buses (Leopard No. 22 and Falcon No. 47) due in for safety checks. Needless to say the engineers were busy that day ensuring that all the vehicles were maintained in first-class condition.

Operations and 24-hour Filling Station

Running a fleet of buses is by no means easy in today's constantly changing operating environment. Maintaining a watchful eye over the stage-carriage operation is the Bus Operations Manager who is assisted by three Operations Assistants. Apart from the day-to-day management of the road staff, the operations staff also deal with enquiries from the general public and are responsible for the efficiency and cost-effectiveness of each of the company's bus routes.

Computers are today helping to ease the load, covering a number of tasks previously carried out manually such as the production of timetables, running boards, crew duties and fare tables, using specialist software from Omnibus Systems helping to save valuable time whilst keeping overheads to a minimum. Other developments include the installation of an electronic cash sorting machine and the introduction of electronic ticket machines. In July 1990, the Wayfarer system replaced the Almex machines introduced in 1987 and provide the operations staff with much quicker production of revenue, management and statistical information.

Outside the offices are the fuel pumps belonging to another aspect of the company's business. The filling station has been operating for around 60 years now and is as much part of the local history as the company's bus services. Today, Maynes continues to pass on the benefits of its bulk-purchasing power on fuel with low-priced petrol and diesel on sale 24 hours a day, seven days a week. The operation of the filling station and shop is also interesting from a financial and accounting point of view, as the running of a relatively expensive garage is spread across two different businesses.

Mayne Coaches

Another garage in the Mayne empire is also open around the clock, but for a very different set of social and economic reasons. The large yard at the company's Fairclough Street coach depot nestles snugly amongst the tall brick railway arches which once carried steam-powered coal trains into the local power station. Nowadays only the local vandals cross the bridge to throw missiles onto the coach fleet below and a security firm is therefore employed to keep watch out-of-hours.

When the company first moved into this former haulier's yard, there was little in the way of office accomodation. Today, however, modern offices house the coach operations and accounts departments along with the company boardroom. Functions carried out here include the monitoring and control of the busy coach operation along with the processing of the company's accounts, including the payroll for both A. Mayne & Son and it associate company Barry Cooper Coaches. Other tasks such as drivers' expenses, the planning of excursions and tours, and tachograph analysis are also carried out here.

The coaching side consists of the long-established holiday express services, as well as an extensive excursions and tours programme. Private hire also forms an increasingly large part of the business along with regular contracts such as prison transfers and education authority work. Mayne's also carry out an increasing amount of conference work and operate regular coach trips for foreign students, taking them to places of interest in connection with their studies.

The 20-strong fleet is therefore quite active throughout the year. Twenty full-time and ten part-time drivers are currently employed and the first coach generally leaves the depot around 07:30. Like the bus division, the coach division also has early and late garage men who ensure that coaches run out on time in addition to working duties themselves. The early garage man arrives at 06:00 and will act as stand-by driver until the late garage man arrives at 14:00. He will then act as the stand-by until 22:00.

Overseeing the operation is the company's Coach Operations Manager who is assisted by the Assistant Coach Manager and a Group Travel Manager. Elsewhere over 40 agents advertise and accept bookings for the company's excursions and tours programme, telephoning all bookings direct to the operations staff at Fairclough Street, with confirmation of acceptance being mailed to the client from there.

On a peak Saturday at the end of July, Maynes' excursions and holiday express service required four coaches and these were being used to operate the four feeder coach routes. Despite servicing as many as 45 pick-up points throughout the area, the company's longest feeder route only takes 55 minutes from end to end and operates from Glossop to Higher Openshaw. All the morning feeders arrived at Mayne Garage at around 08:45 and by 09:05 all four were on their way. Two coaches were off to Blackpool, one across the Pennines to York, the other off along the North Wales coast to Llandudno. A further two coaches would be operating the evening drive to Buxton, after spending the afternoon on a local private hire.

There were 21 private hires in the diary that day and with its existing excursion and contract commitments, the company was hiring in additional vehicles to meet the demand. Whenever they are busy, Maynes will always turn to its associate company for the extra capacity. On this occasion Coopers provided six vehicles, but this still required a seventh coach to be hired in from Le Rad of Romiley, Cheshire.

Another interesting, and prestigious contract occurred a couple of weeks later when one of the Company's Bovas was chartered to take a party of local dignitaries and HRH the Prince of Wales on a tour of the region. In this instance the driving was entrusted to a member of the Royal Protection Squad, though purely for security reasons and not in any way reflecting on Mayne's drivers' capabilities!

The Fleet and the future

There are currently sixteen Leyland coaches in the fleet which are equally split between the Leopard and Tiger chassis. There are also two Bova Futuras which are the flagships of the fleet, and two Dennis Javelins purchased in 1991. The latter are also the newest vehicles to date as investment in recent years has concentrated on increasing the standard of the bus fleet. This might create the impression that the coach side of the business is being run down, but this is certainly not true.

An order has recently been placed for two new Dennis Javelins and these will receive a rather different design from the Wadham Stringer coachwork range. The 55-seaters will be fitted with seat belts and be delivered towards the end of the year, replacing the two Duple-bodied Leyland Tigers delivered in 1989. A third full-specification Bova Futura may also be joining the fleet.

The company's General Manager is also looking with increasing favour on standardising the bus fleet on the Scania L113 and N113, plus Dennis Darts. To help achieve this end the company may consider selling its small fleet of Falcons and also the three Dennis Dominators acquired in 1993. Other vehicles will be replaced gradually when the time is right. Three of the four rebodied Leopards are the next likely candidates for withdrawal. The London Fleetlines are however expected to carry on for a number of years yet and will probably end their lives with Maynes. One DMS in particular has spent the majority of its life with the company having been acquired in 1982.

The Company's operating environment also looks set to change in the near future, not least by GM Buses South's decision to withdraw their competing service 231. The four-year battle with its former associate will come to an end on Saturday 2nd September 1995 , leaving Maynes as the only provider of a bus service between Sunnyside Road and the City centre once more.

Another far-reaching decision is that of Manchester City Council which has decided to reduce the number of bus movements within the City centre. Under the proposals Maynes' bus services will no longer be able to operate through Piccadilly to reach their current terminus at the Arndale Bus Station. Naturally, the company is concerned about the effect this may have on its customers and bus usage as a whole, with the likely disappearance of many important cross-city links.

Within the next ten years the Passenger Transport Authority hopes to obtain powers to extend the City's Metrolink system and Maynes may once again find itself competing with the tram for traffic along Ashton New Road. The proposals are currently in the consultation process and the Company has joined local residents in voicing concern over the issue of on-street running and a likely conflict with pedestrians and other traffic.

History, therefore, looks set to repeat itself yet again and one cannot help wondering what Arthur Mayne would have made of it all. Whatever happens, it is hoped Maynes will continue to prosper and that their loyal customers continue to enjoy travelling the Mayne way.

One of the Company's smart Scania L113s with Northern Counties bodywork, operating on local service 167 shortly before the route was withdrawn on Saturday 2nd September 1995.

A. MAYNE & SON

FLEET HISTORY

KEY:–

Column 1   Fleet number. Where a vehicle has later received a new fleet number it is shown after its original one.

Column 2   Registration number. Where a vehicle has later received a different registration, it is shown in the final 'Notes' column.

Column 3   Chassis details.

Column 4   Bodywork details.

Column 5   Seating capacity & body notation. The first letter shows the type of body:
B – single-deck bus; C – single-deck coach; CH – double-deck bus with coach seating; DP – single-deck dual-purpose (bus/coach; FB – full-fronted single-deck bus (or coach – FC).
The seating capacity is then shown; for double-deckers the split between the two decks is shown, top deck first.
The final letter denotes the entrance position: F – front; C – centre; R – rear; D – dual entrance (front & centre doorways).
Thus H33/29F is double-deck bus with 33 seats upstairs, 29 downstairs and a front entrance.

Column 6   The year the vehicle was first licensed for service.

Column 7   The month and year the vehicle entered the fleet or first ran in service.

Column 8   The month and year the vehicle left the fleet or last ran in service.

f/no.	Reg/n	Chassis Details	Bodywork Details	Seating Capacity	New	In	Out	Notes
1920 - 1928								
		Ford Model-T		B	19	0020		
		AEC Y-type		B	19	0023	0029	
	TW634	AEC 416		B	19	0025?		
	TW1834	AEC 509		B	19	0025?		
1929								

Acquired with the business of J.A. Ferrington, t/a Pioneer Motor Bus Service:

f/no.	Reg/n	Chassis Details	Bodywork Details	Seating Capacity	New	In	Out	Notes
	VM1279	Dennis		FB	19	0029		Later converted to C--
	VM6225	Crossley Eagle	Warwick	B30F	1928	0029		
	VM6226	Crossley Eagle	Warwick	B30F	1928	0029		
	VM6227	Crossley Eagle	Warwick	B30F	1928	0029		
	VR498	AEC Reliance 660		B--F	1929	0029		
1930 - 1932								
	FR8956	Leyland PLC1		C26	1928	0431	0833	Ex Jos Bracewell Ltd
	HD2977	Dennis E		B32F	1927	1032	0735	Ex Yorkshire Woollen (55)
	VH3225	AEC Regal	Duple	C32F	19			Ex Hanson, Huddersfield
	VH3534	AEC Regal	Duple	C32F	19			Ex Hanson, Huddersfield. Rebodied by Duple. Also quoted as VH3541.
1933								
	XJ5574	AEC Regal	Duple	C32R	1933	0033	0053	
	HD3433	Dennis E		B30F	1928	1233	1236	Ex Yorkshire Woollen (95)
1934								
	AXJ496	AEC Regent O661	Park Royal	H32/28F	1934	1134		Later converted to H33/29F
1935								
	BNF553	AEC Regent 0661	Park Royal	H33/29F	1935	0835	0359	Re-bodied by East Lancs to H30/28F in 1945.
	HD2972	Dennis E		B30F	1927	1035	0336	Ex Yorkshire Woollen (53). Scrapped 0736.
1936								
	CNB1	AEC Regent O661	Park Royal	H33/29F	1936	0336	0359	Re-bodied by East Lancs to H30/28F in 1945.
	CVR1	AEC Regent O661	Park Royal	H33/29F	1936	0936	0059	Re-bodied by East Lancs to H30/28F in 1945. Converted to towing wagon 1955.
	SM8353	Albion PKA26		B28F	1930	0736	1139	Ex United A.S AL416. Converted to B20F on del to Mayne
937								
	HD3438	Dennis E		B30F	1928	0337	0637	Ex Yorkshire Woollen (98). Scrapped in 1037.
	DNC156	AEC Regal	Duple	C32F	1937	0037	0939	
	DND3	AEC Regal	Duple	C32F	1937	0037	0040	To Central Ordinance Depot, Chilwell
	DNF2	AEC Regal	Duple	C32F	1937	0037	0040	
	TV735	AEC Regent O661	Park Royal	H33/29F	1930	1237		Ex Nottingham (15). Re-bodied 0038 for Mayne.
938								
	FJ7821	AEC Regent II	Brush	H33/28F	1931	0038		Ex Exeter (23). Re-bodied by East Lancs in 0043.

Thought to have been acquired with the business of J. Bowker and operated separately:

f/no.	Reg/n	Chassis Details	Bodywork Details	Seating Capacity	New	In	Out	Notes
	BNF773	AEC Regal	Duple	C32F	1935	0038		
940								
	FV1686	AEC Regal	Burlingham	C32F	1931	0740	0952	Ex Inman, Morecambe
944								
	AG6021	AEC Regal	Lansdowne (Rebody)	C32F	1931	0044	by 52	Ex Army.
945								
	GND994	Bedford OWB	SMT	B--F				
	TV4491	AEC Regent O661	Park Royal	H28/24R	1931	0945		Acquired from Nottingham (100) for spares.
946								
	TV4945	AEC Regent O661	Park Royal	H28/24R	1931	0446		Acquired from Nottingham (112) for spares. Also quoted as TV4845.
	HNE2	AEC Regal	Santus	C33F	1946	0046	1162	Re-bdy Yeates C39F 0154. F/no alloc 1959. Transferred to Dean fleet 0261.
	HNE3	AEC Regal	Santus	C33F	1946	0046	1162	Re-bdy Yeates C39F 0154. F/no alloc 1959. Transferred to Dean fleet 0361.

f/no.	Reg/n	Chassis Details	Bodywork Details	Seating Capacity	New	In	Out	Notes
1947								
	HF9381	Leyland TD3C	Roe	H48C	1934	0047	0047	Ex Salford (1015), for spares.
	HNE512	Bedford OB	Duple Vista	C29F	1947	0047	0549	
	HXJ566	AEC Regal III O962	Bellhouse Hartwell	C33F	1947	0047	0259	
	HXJ567	AEC Regal III O962	Bellhouse Hartwell	C33F	1947	0047	0259	
1948								
	JNC3	AEC Regal III O962	Bellhouse Hartwell	C33F	1948	0048	1260	
16	JNC4	AEC Regal III O962	Bellhouse Hartwell	C33F	1948	0048	1260	F/no alloc 1959.
	JND404	Bedford OB	Duple Vista	C29F	1948	0048		
1949								
	KNA876	AEC Regent Mk.III	East Lancs	H33/26R	1949	0849	0267	
	KNA877	AEC Regent Mk.III	East Lancs	H33/26R	1949	0949	0267	
17	KVM729	Leyland Tiger PS2	Burlingham	C33F	1949	0049	1260	
1950								
	KVR320	Bedford OB	Duple Vista	C29F	1950	0050	1151	
	AUM407	AEC Regent	Roe (Re-body '46)	H30/26R	1935	0050		Ex Leeds (164).
	AUM434	AEC Regent	Roe	H30/26R	1935	0050	0063	Ex Leeds (191).
	RJ8726	AEC Regent	Metro Cammell	H29/24R	1937	0050	0050	Ex Salford (182). For spares.
1951								
	RJ8728	AEC Regent	Metro Cammell	H28/26R	1938	0051	1261	Ex Salford (184). Scrapped on withdrawal.
1952								
	LXJ318	Bedford SB	Mulliner	C34F	1952	0052		
	DGX214	AEC Regent O661	LPTB	H30/26R	1936	0052	0056	Ex London (STL1694). Scrapped on withdrawal.
1953								
	CUS812	AEC Regent O661	Weymann	H30/26R	1939	0153	0462	Ex Glasgow (647).
	CUS818	AEC Regent O661	Weymann	H30/26R	1939	0153	1263	Ex Glasgow (653).
	MNB717	Bedford SB	Duple Vega	C33F	1953	0053	0056	
	MNC449	Bedford SB	Duple Vega	C33F	1953	0053	0657	
	CXX377	AEC Regent O661	LPTB	H30/26R	1936	1153	00	Ex London (STL1689). For spares.
1954								
1	JGE334	AEC Regal IV	Yeates	C39C	1952	0154	0167	Ex Stewart, Glasgow.
2	HD9304	AEC Regal IV	Plaxton	C41C	1952	0154	1259	Ex Broadhead, Dewsbury.
	7194H	AEC Regent Mk.III 6813S	Park Royal	H32/26R	1953	0854	1072	Former demonstrator. Scrapped on withdrawal.
	DGX210	AEC Regent O661	LPTB	H30/26R	1936	0954	0055	Ex London (STL1679). For spares.
	DGX212	AEC Regent O661	LPTB	H30/26R	1936	1054	0055	Ex London (STL1684). For spares.
14	RVM70	Bedford SBG	Duple Vega	C38F	1954	0054	0063	
1955								
	RNB3	Bedford SBG	Duple Vega	C38F	1955	0055	0756	
	RNB4	Bedford SBG	Duple Vega	C36F	1956	0056	0957	
1956								
8	SVM3	Bedford SBG	Duple Vega	C41F	1956	0456	0163	
9	SVM4	Bedford SBG	Duple Vega	C41F	1956	0456	0063	
10	SVM5	Bedford SBG	Duple Vega	C41F	1956	0456	0063	
	CUS814	AEC Regent	Weymann	H30/26R	1939	0556	1263	Ex Glasgow (649).
3	LBU321	AEC Reliance MU3R	Burlingham	C41C	1955	0756	1266	Ex Holt, Oldham.
1957								

Acquired with the business of F. & H. Dean Ltd, Newton Heath and operated separately:

f/no.	Reg/n	Chassis Details	Bodywork Details	Seating Capacity	New	In	Out	Notes
4	WH3078	Leyland TS1	Harrington (Re-body)	C31F	1931	0357	0458	Acquired by Dean 0740
5	HVU112	Leyland PS1/1	Burlingham	C33F	1947	0357	0061	New to Dean 0847
6	JNE148	Leyland PS1/1	Burlingham	C33F	1948	0357	0961	New to Dean 0648
7	KXJ874	Leyland PS1/1	Burlingham	C33F	1950	0357	0061	New to Dean 0850
8	MVR756	Bedford SB	Duple Vega	C35F	1952	0357	0361	New to Dean 0652
9	RNA632	Bedford SBG	Yeates Riviera III	C36F	1955	0357	0561	New to Dean 0655
	UNF10	AEC Regent Mk.V LD3RA	Park Royal	H41/32R	1957	0757	0077	
	UNF11	AEC Regent Mk.V LD3RA	Park Royal	H41/32R	1957	0757	0674	
	UNF12	AEC Regent Mk.V LD3RA	Park Royal	H41/32R	1957	0757	0674	

f/no.	Reg/n	Chassis Details	Bodywork Details	Seating Capacity	New	In	Out	Notes

1958

| | FT5711 | AEC Regent MK.II | Weymann | H30/26R | 1946 | 1258 | 1267 | Ex Tynemouth (141). |

Acquired with the business of A. Lea, Audenshaw:

| | FV40 | Leyland TS1 | Burlingham (1948) | C33F | 1929 | 1058 | 1058 | Originally Wood Bros. (B/pl) |
| 11 | SVM407 | Bedford SBG | Duple Vega | C41F | 1956 | 1058 | 0063 | New to Lea 0456. |

A 33 seater Seddon (DFV77) was also acquired (and repainted) but never operated by Mayne. It was new to Lea in April 1949.

1959

4	XNB13	Bedford SB1	Duple Super Vega	C41F	1959	0259	0166	
5	XNB14	Bedford SB1	Duple Super Vega	C41F	1959	0259	0267	
6	XNB15	Bedford SB1	Duple Super Vega	C41F	1959	0359	1066	
7	XNB16	Bedford SB1	Duple Super Vega	C41F	1959	0359	0066	Dean fleet from 0662
	XNB17	Bedford SB1	Duple Super Vega	C41F	1959	0359	0268	Dean fleet from new
	GUF678	Leyland Titan PD1	Park Royal	H28/26R	1946	1259	0065	Ex Southdown
15	ATJ511	AEC Regal 662	Plaxton (1949)	FC33F	1936	0359		Ex Empress Coaches

1960

1	2244NA	Bedford SB1	Duple Super Vega	C41F	1960	0060	0167	
2	2245NA	Bedford SB1	Duple Super Vega	C41F	1960	0060	0167	
	ECY874	AEC Regent MK.II	Weymann	H30/26R	1947	0660	1165	Ex South Wales (273).

1961

	4221NC	Bedford SB1	Duple Super Vega	C41F	1961	0261	0968	Dean fleetnames
	6972ND	AEC Regent Mk.V 2D3RA	Park Royal	H41/32R	1961	1261	0076	
	6973ND	AEC Regent Mk.V 2D3RA	Park Royal	H41/32R	1961	1261	0076	
	6974ND	AEC Regent Mk.V 2D3RA	Park Royal	H41/32R	1961	1261	0076	

1962

| | 9085ND | Bedford SB5 | Plaxton Embassy I | C41F | 1962 | 0462 | 1268 | |
| | 9086ND | Bedford SB5 | Plaxton Embassy I | C41F | 1962 | 0462 | 0169 | |

1963

	63DBU	AEC Reliance 4MU3RA	Plaxton Panorama	C51F	1962	0363	0670	Ex demonstrator
	2493VM	Bedford SB5	Plaxton Embassy II	C41F	1963	0463	1169	
	2494VM	Bedford SB5	Plaxton Embassy II	C41F	1963	0463	1169	
	2495VM	Bedford SB5	Plaxton Embassy II	C41F	1963	0463	0569	
	2496VM	Bedford SB5	Plaxton Embassy II	C41F	1963	0463	1170	Dean fleetnames

1964

	291HBU	Bedford SB5	Plaxton Embassy III	C41F	1964	0364	1270	Dean fleetnames
	8859VR	AEC Regent Mk.V 2D3RA	East Lancs	H41/32R	1964	0164		Retired 1180.
	8860VR	AEC Regent Mk.V 2D3RA	East Lancs	H41/32R	1964	0164	1280	Preserved 0081.
	6352VU	AEC Reliance 4MU3RA	Plaxton Panorama	C51F	1964	0364	1171	

1965

	540ETE	Bedford SB8	Yeates Europa	C41F	19	0365	0266	Ex County, Stockport
	BBU958C	Bedford SB5	Plaxton Embassy IV	C41F	1965	0367	0571	Dean fleetnames
	BNF490C	Bedford VAL14	Plaxton Val	C52F	1965	0265	1172	
	BNF491C	Bedford VAL14	Plaxton Val	C52F	1965	0365	0871	
	BNF492C	Bedford VAL14	Plaxton Val	C52F	1965	0565		
	DBU646C	Bedford SB5	Plaxton Panorama	C41F	1965	0665	0072	
	CXJ520C	AEC Regent Mk.V 2D3RA	Neepsend	H41/32R	1965	0865	0078	Scrapped on withdrawal.
	CXJ521C	AEC Regent Mk.V 2D3RA	Neepsend	H41/32R	1965	0865	0078	Scrapped on withdrawal.
	CXJ522C	AEC Regent Mk.V 2D3RA	Neepsend	H41/32R	1965	0865	0078	Scrapped on withdrawal.

1966

| | ENE454D | Bedford VAL14 | Plaxton Val | C52F | 1966 | 0466 | 0075 | |
| | ENE455D | Bedford VAL14 | Plaxton Val | C52F | 1966 | 0466 | 0077 | |

1967

	GNF812E	Bedford VAM14	Plaxton Panorama I	C45F	1964	0367	0474	
	GNF813E	Bedford VAM14	Plaxton Panorama I	C45F	1964	0367	0474	
	GNF814E	Bedford VAM14	Plaxton Panorama I	C45F	1964	0367	1172	

Some of the varied colour schemes carried by Mayne coaches over the years. The basic yet distinctive Plaxton-inspired scheme carried by the early Leopards (as seen on No. 54, facing upper) soon gave way to the more prominent version as applied to the remainder of the batch of Leopards and the last of the Bedfords (as seen on No. 51 facing lower). The later deliveries of Paramount-bodied Tigers carried an even more striking version as seen above; each is slightly different. Following deregulation the buses also adopted a more attractive livery, and the simplified version can be seen below on MRJ 9W, one of the coach-seated VRs. It is operating the Pennine Rambler service 460 from Rochdale and is seen in Stalybridge *en route* to Matlock Bath.

f/no.	Reg/n	Chassis Details	Bodywork Details		Seating Capacity	New	In	Out	Notes
	GNF815E	Bedford VAM14	Plaxton Panorama I	C45F		1964	0367	1172?	
	GNF816E	Bedford VAM14	Plaxton Panorama I	C45F		1964	0367	1172?	
	GNF817E	Bedford VAM14	Plaxton Panorama I	C45F		1964	0367	1172?	

1969

	Reg/n	Chassis Details	Bodywork Details		Seating	New	In	Out	Notes
	LVU885G	Bedford VAL70	Plaxton Panorama Elite	C52F		1969	1169	0077	Ex Mayfair, Wythenshawe.
	TBU7G	Bristol LHL6L	Plaxton Panorama Elite	C51F		1969	0469	1176	
	TBU8G	Bristol LHL6L	Plaxton Panorama Elite	C51F		1969	0469	0576	
	TBU9G	Bristol LHL6L	Plaxton Panorama Elite	C51F		1969	0669	1176	

1970

| | WBU714H | Bristol LH6L | Plaxton Panorama Elite | C45F | | 1970 | 0570 | 0478 | |
| | WBU715H | Bristol LH6L | Plaxton Panorama Elite | C45F | | 1970 | 0570 | 0678 | |

1971

| | BBU37J | Bedford YRQ | Plaxton Panorama Elite II | C45F | | 1971 | 0271 | 0478 | |
| | BBU38J | Bedford YRQ | Plaxton Panorama Elite II | C45F | | 1971 | 0271 | 0480 | |

Acquired with the business of R. Connolly Ltd, Gorton:

| | MVM824G | Bedford VAL70 | Plaxton Panorama Elite | C52F | | 1969 | 1071 | | New to Connolly 0669. |

1972

	FBU300K	Bedford YRQ	Plaxton Panorama Elite II	C45F		1972	0372	0678	
	FBU301K	Bedford YRQ	Plaxton Panorama Elite II	C45F		1972	0372	0078	
	FBU302K	AEC Reliance 6U3ZR	Plaxton Elite Express II	C51F		1972	0572	0280	
	FBU303K	AEC Reliance 6U3ZR	Plaxton Elite Express II	C51F		1972	0572	0079	
	FBU304K	AEC Reliance 6U3ZR	Plaxton Elite Express II	C51F		1972	0572	1280	
	FBU305K	AEC Reliance 6U3ZR	Plaxton Elite Express II	C51F		1972	0572	1078	

1973

	LBU701L	Bedford SB5	Plaxton Panorama IV	C41F		1973	0373	0680	
	LBU702L	Bedford SB5	Plaxton Panorama IV	C41F		1973	0373	0279	
	LBU703L	Bedford SB5	Plaxton Panorama IV	C41F		1973	0573	0579	
	LBU704L	Bedford SB5	Plaxton Panorama IV	C41F		1973	0573	0679	

1974

| | WVU829L | Ford Transit | Williams | C12F | | 1973 | 1274 | 0382? | Ex Wilson, Failsworth |

Acquired with the business of E. Morby & Sons Ltd, Droylsden and operated separately:

| | FYG775C | Bedford SB5 | Duple | C41F | | 1965 | 0074 | 0077? | In to Morby 0268 |
| | KTJ669C | Bedford VAL14 | Plaxton Val | C52F | | 1965 | 0074 | 0077 | In to Morby 0671 |

1975

	HBA696N	Bedford YRT	Plaxton Panorama Elite III	C53F		1975	0275	0081	
	KVU60P	Bedford YRT	Plaxton Panorama Elite III	C53F		1975	1275	0480	
	KVU61P	Bedford YRT	Plaxton Panorama Elite III	C53F		1975	1275	0480	
	KVU62P	Bedford YRT	Plaxton Panorama Elite III	C53F		1975	1275	0880	

1976

10	LRJ210P	Daimler Fleetline CRG6LXB	Roe	H44/34F		1976	0676	1190	Scrapped on withdrawal.
11	LRJ211P	Daimler Fleetline CRG6LXB	Roe	H44/34F		1976	0676	0087	Scrapped on withdrawal.
12	LRJ212P	Daimler Fleetline CRG6LXB	Roe	H44/34F		1976	0676	1188	
13	LRJ213P	Daimler Fleetline CRG6LXB	Roe	H44/34F		1976	0676	1088	
14	LRJ214P	Daimler Fleetline CRG6LXB	Roe	H44/34F		1976	0676	0988	
	JCU800G	Ford R226	Duple Northern Viceroy	C53F		1969	0676	1276	Ex Wilson, Failsworth.

1977

	SBA199R	Bedford YMT	Plaxton Supreme	C53F		1977	0577	0081	
	SBA200R	Bedford YMT	Plaxton Supreme	C53F		1977	0677	0680	
	SBA201R	Bedford YMT	Plaxton Supreme	C53F		1977	0677	0881	
	SBA202R	Bedford VAS5	Plaxton Supreme	C29F		1977	0777	0081	

1978

	VJA660S	Bedford YMT	Plaxton Supreme	C53F		1978	0178	0782	
	VJA661S	Bedford YMT	Plaxton Supreme	C53F		1978	0178	0882	
	VJA663S	Bedford SB5	Plaxton Supreme	C41F		1978	0378	0384	

f/no.	Reg/n	Chassis Details	Bodywork Details	Seating Capacity	New	In	Out	Notes
	VJA664S	Bedford SB5	Plaxton Supreme	C41F	1978	0478	0882	
15	VJA665S	Bristol VRT/SL3/6LXB	Eastern Coach Works	CH41/29F	1978	0678	0789	
16	VJA666S	Bristol VRT/SL3/6LXB	Eastern Coach Works	CH41/29F	1978	0478	1089	
17	VJA667S	Bristol VRT/SL3/6LXB	Eastern Coach Works	CH41/29F	1978	0678	0789	
	YNF347T	Bedford YMT	Plaxton Supreme IV	C53F	1978	0078	0582	Was intended to be VJA662S
	YNF348T	Bedford YMT	Plaxton Supreme IV	C53F	1978	0878	1181	
	YNF349T	Bedford YMT	Plaxton Supreme IV	C53F	1978	1278		
	YNF350T	Bedford SB5	Duple Dominant I	C41F	1978	1278	0984	
	YNF351T	Bedford SB5	Duple Dominant I	C41F	1978	1278	0483	

1979

f/no.	Reg/n	Chassis Details	Bodywork Details	Seating Capacity	New	In	Out	Notes
	TNE14K	Bedford SB5	Plaxton Panorama III	C41F	1972	0779	0979	Ex R. Wood & Sons
	TNE15K	Bedford SB5	Plaxton Panorama III	C41F	1972	0779	1079	Ex R. Wood & Sons

1980

f/no.	Reg/n	Chassis Details	Bodywork Details	Seating Capacity	New	In	Out	Notes
	HDB352V	Bedford YMT	Plaxton Supreme IV	C53F	1980	0280	0282	
	HDB353V	Bedford YMT	Plaxton Supreme IV	C53F	1980	0280	0282	
54	HDB354V	Leyland Leopard PSU3F/5R	Plaxton Supreme IV	C53F	1980	0280	0986	Became LJX139 in 0286. To Barry Cooper
55	HDB355V	Leyland Leopard PSU3F/5R	Plaxton Supreme IV	C53F	1980	0280	0887	Became NMX643 in 0286 To Barry Cooper
56	HDB356V	Leyland Leopard PSU5C/4R	Plaxton Supreme IV	C57F	1980	0580	0785	Became 289BUA in 1185. To Barry Cooper
57	HDB357V	Leyland Leopard PSU5C/4R	Plaxton Supreme IV	C57F	1980	0580	0785	Became 906GAU in 1185. To Barry Cooper
58/66	MRJ358W	Leyland Leopard PSU3F/4R	Plaxton Supreme IV Express	C53F	1980	0680		Became MJI5766 in 0290
8	MRJ8W	Bristol VRT/SL3/6LXB	Eastern Coach Works	CH41/29F	1980	0780	0191	
9	MRJ9W	Bristol VRT/SL3/6LXB	Eastern Coach Works	CH41/29F	1980	0780	0191	

1981

f/no.	Reg/n	Chassis Details	Bodywork Details	Seating Capacity	New	In	Out	Notes
	LDJ723W	Mercedes L207D	Devon	C12F	1981	0881	0487	Ex O'Brien, Farnworth
59	MRJ359W	Leyland Leopard PSU5C/4R	Plaxton Supreme IV	C57F	1981	0481		Became GIL3259 in 0490
60	MRJ360W	Leyland Leopard PSU5C/4R	Plaxton Supreme IV	C57F	1981	0481		Became GIL2160 in 0390
61	SNC361X	Leyland Leopard PSU5C/4R	Plaxton Supreme IV	C57F	1981	0881	0291	Became NIB3261 in 0190. To Barry Cooper
64	SNC364X	Leyland Leopard PSU5C/4R	Plaxton Supreme IV	C50F	1981	0881		Became MJI5764 in 0290. Later converted to C57F

1982

f/no.	Reg/n	Chassis Details	Bodywork Details	Seating Capacity	New	In	Out	Notes
52	SND352X	Leyland Tiger TRCTL11/3R	Plaxton Supreme VI Express	C53F	1982	0382	1089	
53	SND353X	Leyland Tiger TRCTL11/3R	Plaxton Supreme VI Express	C53F	1982	0382	1089	
62	SNC362X	Leyland Leopard PSU5C/4R	Plaxton Supreme IV	C57F	1982	0482		Became NIB4162 in 0490
66	SNC366X	Leyland Leopard PSU3A/4R	Plaxton Supreme IV	C53F	1970	0482	0386	Was WHA236H, re-bodied. To Barry Cooper.
65	SNC365X	Leyland Leopard PSU5C/4R	Plaxton Supreme IV	C57F	1982	0682		Became MJI5765 in 0290
	PTO350R	Leyland Leopard PSU5A/4R	Plaxton Supreme III	C57F	1976	0682	0583	To Barry Cooper
63	SNC363X	Leyland Leopard PSU5C/4R	Plaxton Supreme IV	C57F	1982	0782		Became MJI5763 in 0290
3	OJD163R	Leyland Fleetline FE30AGR	Park Royal	H44/29F	1976	1282		Ex LT (DM2163) via Stevensons (as dealers)

1983

f/no.	Reg/n	Chassis Details	Bodywork Details	Seating Capacity	New	In	Out	Notes
67	ANA367Y	Leyland Tiger TRCTL11/3R	Plaxton Paramount 3500 Exp	C55F	1983	0383	0293	Became OJT923 in 0386
68/69	ANA368Y	Leyland Tiger TRCTL11/3R	Plaxton Paramount 3500 Exp	C55F	1983	0383		Became SSV269 in 0386

1984

f/no.	Reg/n	Chassis Details	Bodywork Details	Seating Capacity	New	In	Out	Notes
51	A351KBA	Bedford PJK	Plaxton Supreme IV	C29F	1984	0484	1190	To Barry Cooper. Became CSU918 in 0991.
69	A369HNC	Leyland Tiger TRCTL11/3R	Plaxton Paramount 3500	C49F	1984	0384	0086	Became SXU708 by 0186
70	A370HNC	Leyland Tiger TRCTL11/3R	Plaxton Paramount 3500	C49Ft	1983	0983		Became TKU540 in 1185

1985

f/no.	Reg/n	Chassis Details	Bodywork Details	Seating Capacity	New	In	Out	Notes
1	OJD131R	Leyland Fleetline FE30AGR	Park Royal	H44/29F	1976	0185	0594	Ex Stevensons, Uttoxeter. To Barry Cooper
5	OUC35R	Leyland Fleetline FE30AGR	Metro Cammell Weymann	H45/32F	1976	0385	0595	Ex Barry Cooper. Scrapped on withdrawal.
49/79	B349RNA	Leyland Tiger TRCTLXCT/3RZ	Plaxton Paramount 3200II	C57F	1985	0585		Became LIB6439 in 1088
50	B350RNA	Leyland Tiger TRCTLXCT/3RZ	Plaxton Paramount 3200II	C57F	1985	0585		Became 403BGO in 0687

1986

f/no.	Reg/n	Chassis Details	Bodywork Details	Seating Capacity	New	In	Out	Notes
47/77	C347YBA	Leyland Tiger TRCTLXCT/3RZ	Plaxton Paramount 3500 II	C51Ft	1986	0386		Became LIB6437 in 1088
48/78	C348YBA	Leyland Tiger TRCTLXCT/3RZ	Plaxton Paramount 3500 II	C51Ft	1986	0386		Became LIB6438 in 0988
54	ORO325L	Leyland Leopard PSU5/4R	Duple 320 (1986)	C57F	1973	0986		Ex Barry Cooper. Sent to Duple and returned as ASV764 in 1186. Fitted with TL11 218bhp engine.

1987

f/no.	Reg/n	Chassis Details	Bodywork Details	Seating Capacity	New	In	Out	Notes
	SCP342L	Leyland Leopard PSU4B/2R	Plaxton Derwent	B45F	1973	0387	1087	Ex WYT(3002). Did not enter service. To Barry Cooper
6	UJX916M	Leyland Leopard PSU4B/2R	Plaxton Derwent	B45F	1973	0387	0488	Ex WYT(3006). To Barry Cooper.
4	UJX918M	Leyland Leopard PSU4B/2R	Plaxton Derwent	B45F	1973	0387	1188	Ex WYT(3008). To Barry Cooper.
2	GWY692N	Leyland Leopard PSU4B/2R	Plaxton Derwent	B43F	1975	0387	1288	Ex WYT(3012)
7	JWU252N	Leyland Leopard PSU4C/4R	Plaxton Derwent	B43F	1975	0387	1288	Ex WYT(8509). To Barry Cooper 0189.
55	GRF267V	Leyland Leopard PSU3E/4R	Duple Dominant II Express	C53F	1980	0587	1287	Ex Barry Cooper. Returned to Barry Cooper.
18	LJA474P	Daimler Fleetline CRG6LXB	Northern Counties	H43/32F	1975	0787	0993	Ex GMT(7474)

The change from the traditional maroon and turquoise bus livery began with the delivery of the first coach-seated VRs, in 1978. Regent V 8860 VR, now preserved in the Museum of Transport, was posed alongside newly delivered (and much photographed) VJA 666S at the Sunnyside Road terminus. The Roe-bodied Fleetlines were the last vehicles to be delivered in the old livery – until the 75th Anniversary vehicle – and both liveries can be seen on this page. The turquiouse scheme was progressively replaced as these vehicles became due for repaint.

Former London Fleetline OJD 163R began its life in exile in December 1982 and was joined three years later by two more ex-patriots. By this time the vehicles had adopted fleet numbers and number 1 can be seen below in the Stevenson-inspired livery, leaving the appropriately named Stevenson Square. Number 3 (above) continued to sport the standard colour scheme and was photographed whilst approaching the Mayne garage on a short working. Just for good measure the third member, number 5, was completely different .

f/no.	Reg/n	Chassis Details	Bodywork Details	Seating Capacity	New	In	Out	Notes
11	LJA470P	Daimler Fleetline CRG6LXB	Northern Counties	H43/32F	1975	1087	0893	Ex GMT(7470)
19	GWY691N	Leyland Leopard PSU4B/2R	Plaxton Derwent	DP43F	1975	1087	1288	Ex WYT(3011) via Barry Cooper.

1988

f/no.	Reg/n	Chassis Details	Bodywork Details	Seating Capacity	New	In	Out	Notes
22/8	YNA328M	Daimler Fleetline CRG6LXB	Northern Counties	H43/32F	1973	0088	0994	Ex GMT(7373). Scrapped on withdrawal.
20	BNE735N	Daimler Fleetline CRG6LXB	Northern Counties	H43/32F	1974	0888	0794	Ex GMT(7419)
19	BNE740N	Daimler Fleetline CRG6LXB	Northern Counties	H43/32F	1974	0088	0091	Ex GMT(7424). Entered service 0889?
6	GNC294N	Daimler Fleetline CRG6LXB	Northern Counties	H43/32F	1974	0088	0092	Ex GMT(7428)
4	GND505N	Daimler Fleetline CRG6LXB	Northern Counties	H43/32F	1974	0088	0794	Ex GMT(7439). To Barry Cooper.
14	GND507N	Daimler Fleetline CRG6LXB	Northern Counties	H43/32F	1974	0088	0292	Ex GMT(7441). Low bridge accident
55	GRF267V	Leyland Leopard PSU3E/4R	Duple Dominant II Express	C53F	1980	1088	0389	Returned to Barry Cooper.
21	WWH54L	Daimler Fleetline CRG6LXB	Northern Counties	H43/32F	1973	1288	0391	Ex GMT(7289)
	WWH62L	Daimler Fleetline CRG6LXB	Northern Counties	H43/32F	1973	1188	0088	Ex Smiths, Alcester. For spares.
	YNA306M	Daimler Fleetline CRG6LXB	Northern Counties	H43/32F	1973	1188	0088	Ex GMT(7351). For spares.
	YNA315M	Daimler Fleetline CRG6LXB	Northern Counties	H43/32F	1973	1188	0088	Ex London, Harrow. For spares.
23	NTX361R	Leyland Leopard PSU3C/2R	Willowbrook	B51F	1976	1188	0291	Ex Merthyr Tydfil. Became LIW1324 in 1090
24/25	NTX362R	Leyland Leopard PSU3C/2R	Willowbrook	B51F	1976	1188		Ex Merthyr Tydfil. Entered service 0189. Became NIB7625 in 1090 with Warrior bodywork in 0391.
25	NTX363R	Leyland Leopard PSU3C/2R	Willowbrook	B51F	1976	1188	0291	Ex Merthyr Tydfil. To Barry Cooper.

1989

f/no.	Reg/n	Chassis Details	Bodywork Details	Seating Capacity	New	In	Out	Notes
69	UWY62X	Leyland Leopard PSU3C/4R	Duple Dominant IV Express	C57F	1982	0189	0190	Ex West Yorkshire.
55	F55HNC	Leyland Tiger TRCL10/3ARZM	Duple 340	C53Ft	1989	0189		Became IIL1355 in 0092.
56	F56HNC	Leyland Tiger TRCTL11/3RZA	Duple 320	C57F	1989	0189		Became IIL1356 in 0092.
	WWH24L	Daimler Fleetline CRG6LXB	Park Royal	H43/32F	1973	0289	0089	Ex Council for Social Aid, Sale. For spares.
	NTX360R	Leyland Leopard PSU3C/2R	Willowbrook	B51F	1976	0389	0089	Ex Merthyr Tydfil. For spares.
12	F112HNC	Scania N113DRB	Northern Counties	H47/32F	1989	0389		
	XJA542L	Daimler Fleetline CRG6LXB	Park Royal	H43/32F	1973	0489	0089	Ex Gash, Newark. For spares.
13	F113HNC	Scania N113DRB	Northern Counties	CH47/30F	1989	0589		
	C518WBF	Leyland Tiger TRCL11/3RZ	Duple 340	C50Ft	1986	0589	0889	Ex Midland Red South (31)
	C520WBF	Leyland Tiger TRCL11/3RZ	Duple 340	C50Ft	1986	0589	0290	Ex Midland Red South (32). To Barry Cooper, becoming FIL9386 in 0290.
2	CSU918	Daimler Fleetline CRG6LXB	Northern Counties	H43/32F	1974	0889	1091	Ex Hulme Hall Coaches. Previously XJA566L, becoming DRJ917L in 0991
69/24	OWO234Y	Leyland Leopard PSU3G/2R	Duple Dominant	DP49F	1982	1189	0493	Ex Merthyr Tydfil
15	G115SBA	Scania N113DRB	Northern Counties	H47/32F	1989	1089		
16	G116SBA	Scania N113DRB	Northern Counties	H47/32F	1989	1289		

1990

f/no.	Reg/n	Chassis Details	Bodywork Details	Seating Capacity	New	In	Out	Notes
17	G117SBA	Scania N113DRB	Northern Counties	H47/32F	1989	0290		
57	G57SBA	Bova FHD 12.290	Bova Futura	C50Ft	1990	0290		Became IIL2257 in 0892
58	G58SBA	Bova FHD 12.290	Bova Futura	C50Ft	1990	0390		Became IIL2258 in 0892. Now C40Ft with tables.
7/27/41	GDZ3841	Leyland Leopard PSU3B/4R	Willowbrook Warrior (1990)	B51F	1975	0290		Was JVS928N. Ex Perry, Bromyard
22	NRE582L	Leyland Leopard PSU3B/4R	Willowbrook Warrior (1990)	B48F	1973	0590		Acquired as a chassis, becoming LIW1322 in 1090. Re-bodied in 1290.
23	RBF987M	Leyland Leopard PSU3B/4R	Willowbrook Warrior (1990)	B48F	1973	0590		Acquired as a chassis, becoming LIW1323 in 1090. Re-bodied in 1290.
	LBF796P	Leyland Leopard PSU3C/4R			1975	0590	0090	Acquired as a chassis and scrapped for spares.
10	KUC969P	Leyland Fleetline FE30AGR	Metro Cammell Weymann	H45/32F	1976	1190	0794	Ex Wilts & Dorset. Converted to 6LXB by Mayne. To Barry Cooper 0794.

1991

f/no.	Reg/n	Chassis Details	Bodywork Details	Seating Capacity	New	In	Out	Notes
26	SSX601V	Seddon Pennine VII	Alexander AYS	B53F	1980	0191	0893	Ex Stevensons, Uttoxeter.
21	A101DPB	Dennis Falcon HS SDA407	Wadham Stringer Vanguard (1987)	DP49F	1983	0191		Ex Berks Bucks.
	THX496S	Leyland Fleetine FE30ALR Special	Park Royal	H44/24D	1978	0391	0091	For spares (was LT DMS2496)
28/33	THX303S	Leyland Fleetine FE30ALR Special	Metro Cammell Weymann	H44/31F	1978	0391	0795	Was LT (DMS2303). Accident victim.
7	THX322S	Leyland Fleetine FE30ALR Special	Metro Cammell Weymann	H44/31F	1978	0391		Was LT (DMS2322).
9	THX579S	Leyland Fleetine FE30ALR Special	Park Royal	H44/27F	1978	0391		Was LT (DMS2579).
35/2	THX515S	Leyland Fleetine FE30ALR Special	Park Royal	H44/31F	1978	0391		Was LT (DMS2515).
29/35	THX555S	Leyland Fleetine FE30ALR Special	Park Royal	H44/31F	1978	0391		Was LT (DMS2555).
34	THX594S	Leyland Fleetine FE30ALR Special	Park Royal	H44/31F	1978	0391		Was LT (DMS2594).
31	THX601S	Leyland Fleetine FE30ALR Special	Park Royal	H44/31F	1978	0391		Was LT (DMS2601).
51	H51DVR	Dennis Javelin 8.5 SDA1915	Duple 320	C37F	1991	0391		Later converted to C35F.
52	H52FDB	Dennis Javelin 12 SDL1907	Duple 320	C57F	1991	0491		
53	D323RNS	Leyland Tiger TRCTL11/3R	Duple 340	C46Ft	1987	0991	0994	Ex Highland Scottish, becoming HIL6253 in 1291.

f/no.	Reg/n	Chassis Details	Bodywork Details	Seating Capacity	New	In	Out	Notes
44	A44YWJ	Dennis Falcon HS SDA414	Marshall Camair-80	DP53F	1983	1191		Ex Chesterfield
45	A45YWJ	Dennis Falcon HS SDA414	Marshall Camair-80	B53F	1983	1191		Ex Chesterfield
46	A46YWJ	Dennis Falcon HS SDA414	Marshall Camair-80	B53F	1983	1191		Ex Chesterfield
47	A47YWJ	Dennis Falcon HS SDA414	Marshall Camair-80	B53F	1983	1191		Ex Chesterfield
48	A48YWJ	Dennis Falcon HS SDA414	Marshall Camair-80	B53F	1983	1191		Ex Chesterfield

1992

f/no.	Reg/n	Chassis Details	Bodywork Details	Seating Capacity	New	In	Out	Notes
	THX564S	Leyland Fleetine FE30ALR Special	Park Royal	H44/24D	1978	0292	0092	For spares (was LT DMS2496).
19	THX619S	Leyland Fleetine FE30ALR Special	Park Royal	H44/31F	1978	0292		Was LT (DMS2619).
	THX623S	Leyland Fleetine FE30ALR Special	Park Royal	H44/24D	1978	0292	0092	For spares (was LT DMS2623).
	THX635S	Leyland Fleetine FE30ALR Special	Park Royal	H44/24D	1978	0292	0092	For spares (was LT DMS2635).
32	GSC857T	Leyland Fleetine FE30AGR	Eastern Coach Works	H43/32F	1979	1192		Ex Clydeside 2000
6	ULS666T	Leyland Fleetine FE30AGR	Eastern Coach Works	H43/32F	1979	1192		Ex Clydeside 2000.
28	K28XBA	Dennis Dart 9.8 SDL3035	Marshall Dartline	B40F	1992	1192		
30	ULS663T	Leyland Fleetine FE30AGR	Eastern Coach Works	H43/32F	1979	1292		Ex Clydeside 2000.

1993

f/no.	Reg/n	Chassis Details	Bodywork Details	Seating Capacity	New	In	Out	Notes
29	K29XBA	Dennis Dart 9.8 SDL3035	Marshall Dartline	B40F	1993	0193		
36	K36XNE	Dennis Dominator DDA2005	East Lancs	H45/31F	1993	0393		Originally allocated K216OGD for Strathclyde
37	K37XNE	Dennis Dominator DDA2005	East Lancs	H45/31F	1993	0393		Originally allocated K217OGD for Strathclyde
38	K38YVM	Dennis Dominator DDA2005	East Lancs	H45/31F	1993	0393		Originally allocated K218OGD for Strathclyde

1994

f/no.	Reg/n	Chassis Details	Bodywork Details	Seating Capacity	New	In	Out	Notes
14	L114DNA	Scania N113DRB	East Lancs	H47/31F	1993	0893		Was intended to be K114XNE
26	L26FNE	Dennis Dart 9.8 SDL3035	Marshall Dartline	B40F	1993	0294		Del 270194.
27	L27FNE	Dennis Dart 9.8 SDL3035	Marshall Dartline	B40F	1993	0294		Del 280194.
	ARB134T	Leyland Leopard PSU3E/4R	Plaxton Supreme Express	C49F	1978	0894	0994	Ex Trent (1134). To Barry Cooper.
	BRC140T	Leyland Leopard PSU3E/4R	Plaxton Supreme Express	C49F	1979	0894	0994	Ex Trent (1140). To Barry Cooper.
24	KVO144W	Leyland Leopard PSU3E/4R	Willowbrook 003	C49F	1980	0894		Ex Trent (144).
40	KVO145W	Leyland Leopard PSU3E/4R	Willowbrook 003	C49F	1981	0894		Ex Trent (145). Stored until 0794. Entered service 010895.
	KVO146W	Leyland Leopard PSU3E/4R	Willowbrook 003	C49F	1981	0894		Ex Trent (146). Body removed 1294.

Another 19 Leyland Leopards were also acquired from Trent/Barton, the majority of which were immediately sold on. They were as follows:

RVO655/64/71L, XRR612/7/8/21M, OAL620M, OMN275/82M, PNN767/71/3/4M, GNN214N - all PSU3B/4Rs with Plaxton Panorama Elite III Express coachwork.
KVO142W - a PSU3E/4R with Willowbrook 003 coachwork.
SCH149/51X and VNN54Y - PSU3F/4Rs also with Willowbrook 003 coachwork.

f/no.	Reg/n	Chassis Details	Bodywork Details	Seating Capacity	New	In	Out	Notes
	THX593S	Leyland Fleetline FE30ALR	Park Royal	H44/27D	1978	1194		Ex Arkleston, Renfew. For spares.
42	M42ONF	Scania L113CRL	Northern Counties Paladin	B51F	1994	1194		
43	M113RNK	Scania L113CRL	Northern Counties Paladin	B49F	1994	1294		Ex demonstrator.

1995

f/no.	Reg/n	Chassis Details	Bodywork Details	Seating Capacity	New	In	Out	Notes
10	M210NDB	Scania N113DRB	East Lancs	H45/31F	1995	0295		
11	M211NDB	Scania N113DRB	East Lancs	H45/31F	1995	0295		
	UWY80X	Leyland Leopard PSU3F/4R	Duple Dominant IV Express	C49F	1981	0495	0695?	Ex Yorkshire Rider (1549)

BARRY COOPER COACHES/THE MAYNE GROUP:

The fleet acquired in January 1982:

f/no.	Reg/n	Chassis Details	Bodywork Details	Seating Capacity	New	In	Out	Notes
	UEB464K	Leyland Leopard PSU3B/4RT	Plaxton Panorama Elite II	C51F	1972	0175	0483	
11	SCK869	Leyland Leopard PSU3/3RT	Plaxton Panorama Elite III	C49F	1962	0575	0290	Re-bodied from Duple. Ex PMT (19). Converted to C53F in 0785 and became ACA642A in 1186.
7	JTB869P	Leyland Leopard PSU5A/4R	Plaxton Panorama Elite III	C57F	1975	0975	0287	Became 480XYB in 0187.
	MEK212P	Leyland Leopard PSU3C/4R	Plaxton Supreme III	C53F	1976	0376	0585	
	ODJ51R	Leyland Leopard PSU3C/4R	Plaxton Supreme III	C53F	1976	0876	0585	
	PJP275R	Leyland Leopard PSU3/4R	Plaxton Supreme III	C53F	1963	0377	0586	Previously 91FXD. Re-bodied by Coopers in 0077.
	PJP276R	Leyland Leopard L2T	Plaxton Supreme III	C45F	1961	0477	0586	Previously MCN56. Re-bodied by Coopers in 0077.
	BUN457L	Leyland Leopard PSU3B/4R	Plaxton Panorama Elite III	C53F	1973	0478	1283	
14	VJP391S	Leyland Leopard L2T	Plaxton Supreme III	C45F	1961	0478	0089	Previously MCN61. Re-bodied by Coopers in 0078.
	AED132T	Leyland Leopard PSU5B/4R	Plaxton Viewmaster	C57F	1978	0878	1183	
	TGD992R	Volvo B58-56	Plaxton Viewmaster		1977	1278	0384	
13	BJP642T	Leyland Leopard PSU4/4R	Plaxton Supreme IV (Rebody)	C45F	1966	0479	0390	Previously FJA227D
	DED571T	Leyland Leopard PSU5C/4R	Plaxton Supreme IV	C57F	1979	0779	0685	
	EFM96S	Leyland Leopard PSU3/4R	Plaxton Supreme III	C51F	1964	0979	0586	Previously AAD242B

Mayne's recent second-hand purchases have included many different and interesting machines. With deregulation came the arrival of surplus Fleetlines from the neighbouring PTE, whilst similarly redundant single-deck Leopards came from the West Yorkshire PTE. Former GMT 7417, soon to be Mayne's number 11, is seen on previous home territory in Tintwistle, whilst Yorkshire Pudding number 2 was posed on service 394 from Lane Ends to Hazel Grove. More recent acquisitions include Fleetlines from Clydeside 2000 and ex-Chesterfield Falcons with Marshall Camair bodies. Both can be seen on Manor Road, Droylsden.

Two of Maynes Northern Counties-bodied Scanias at work in August 1995.

f/no.	Reg/n	Chassis Details	Bodywork Details	Seating Capacity	New	In	Out	Notes
12	XND4L	Leyland Leopard PSU5C/4R	Plaxton Panorama Elite III	C57F	1973	0380	0587	Became 974EYB by 0986.
	JEK121V	Volvo B58-61	Plaxton Viewmaster IV	C57F	1980	0380	0583	
17	ODJ417W	Leyland Leopard PSU5D/4R	Plaxton Supreme IV	C57F	1981	0381		Became VGU443 in 1282
	OJP908W	Leyland Leopard PSU3A/4R	Duple Dominant III (Rebody)	C53F	1970	0481	1183	Previously WHA252H
	DFM881X	Leyland Leopard PSU3A/4R	Duple Dominant III (Rebody)	C53F	1970	0881	0584	Previously WHA229H
	TKW723S	Volvo B58-61	Plaxton Viewmaster	C53F	1978	1081	1083	

1983

f/no.	Reg/n	Chassis Details	Bodywork Details	Seating Capacity	New	In	Out	Notes
10	PTO350R	Leyland Leopard PSU5A/4R	Plaxton Supreme III	C57F	1976	0583	0091	Ex Mayne. Became UCE665 in 1185
18	A418HND	Leyland Tiger TRCTL11/3R	Plaxton Paramount 3200	C57F	1983	0883		Became YPL764 in 1185
19	A419HND	Leyland Tiger TRCTL11/3R	Duple Laser	C57F	1983	0983		Became YUC765 in 1185

1984

f/no.	Reg/n	Chassis Details	Bodywork Details	Seating Capacity	New	In	Out	Notes
23	A423LRJ	Leyland Tiger TRCTL11/3R	Plaxton Paramount 3200	C53F	1984	0184	0091	Became 614BWU in 1185
22	A422KBA	Bedford PJK	Plaxton Supreme IV	C29F	1984	0284	1190	Became UCE665 in 0590, then A609XFM in 1090
20	A420HND	Leyland Tiger TRCTL11/3R	Plaxton Paramount 3500	C57F	1984	0484	0187	Became 507EXA in 0386
21	A421KBA	Leyland Tiger TRCTL11/3R	Plaxton Paramount 3500	C53Ft	1984	0484		Became EUK978 in 0386

1985

f/no.	Reg/n	Chassis Details	Bodywork Details	Seating Capacity	New	In	Out	Notes
	OUC35R	Leyland Fleetline FE30AGR	Metro Cammell Weymann	H45/32F	1976	0085	0385	Ex Happy Days, Woodseaves. To Mayne.
24	B424RNA	Leyland Tiger TRCTL11/3R	Plaxton Paramount 3200II	C53F	1985	0385		Became OED201 in 1185
25	B425RNA	Leyland Tiger TRCTL11/3R	Plaxton Paramount 3200II	C57F	1985	0385		Became UOL337 in 1185
56/16	IIDB356V	Leyland Leopard PSU5C/4R	Plaxton Supreme IV	C57F	1980	0785		Ex Mayne. Became 289BUA in 1185
57/15	HDB357V	Leyland Leopard PSU5C/4R	Plaxton Supreme IV	C57F	1980	0785		Ex Mayne. Became 906GAU in 1185
	ORO325L	Leyland Leopard PSU5/4R	Van Hool Vistadome	C57F	1973	0785	0986	To Mayne via Duple for rebodying.

1986

f/no.	Reg/n	Chassis Details	Bodywork Details	Seating Capacity	New	In	Out	Notes
66	SNC366X	Leyland Leopard PSU3A/4R	Plaxton Supreme IV	C53F	1970	0386		Ex Mayne. Previously WHA236H, becoming UCE665 by 0593
26	C426YBA	Leyland Tiger TRCTLXCT/3RZ	Plaxton Paramount 3500 II	C51F	1986	0386		Became LIB6440 in 1088
11	UTU23V	Leyland Tiger TRCTL11/2RSp	Duple Dominant II	C49F	1980	0386	0092	Ex Leyland (Test Rig). First reg 0986. Became SCK869 in 1186
54	LJX139	Leyland Leopard PSU5C/4R	Plaxton Supreme IV	C57F	1980	0486	0893	Ex Mayne (HDB354V)
		Leyland Titan TNLX--/	Park Royal	H--/--F		0086	0086	Prototype. For spares only.

1987

f/no.	Reg/n	Chassis Details	Bodywork Details	Seating Capacity	New	In	Out	Notes
	XBF59S	Leyland Leopard PSU3E/4R	Duple Dominant I Express	C49F	1978	0187	0387	Ex PMT (59).
	XBF62S	Leyland Leopard PSU3E/4R	Duple Dominant I Express	C49F	1978	0187	0087	Ex PMT (62).
	XBF63S	Leyland Leopard PSU3E/4R	Duple Dominant I Express	C49F	1978	0187	0087	Ex PMT (63).
	GRF265V	Leyland Leopard PSU3E/4R	Duple Dominant II Express	C53F	1980	0187	0189	Ex PMT (65).
	GRF267V	Leyland Leopard PSU3E/4R	Duple Dominant II Express	C53F	1980	0187	0587	Ex PMT (67). To Mayne.
	GRF268V	Leyland Leopard PSU3E/4R	Duple Dominant II Express	C53F	1980	0187	0087	Ex PMT (68).
3	SCP343L	Leyland Leopard PSU4B/2R	Plaxton Derwent	B45F	1973	0387	0188	Ex WYT(3003)
4	SCP344L	Leyland Leopard PSU4B/2R	Plaxton Derwent	B45F	1973	0387	0188	Ex WYT(3004)
5	SCP345L	Leyland Leopard PSU4B/2R	Plaxton Derwent	B45F	1973	0387	1187	Ex WYT(3005)
	GWY691N	Leyland Leopard PSU4B/2R	Plaxton Derwent	DP43F	1975	0387	1087	Ex WYT(3011). To Mayne.
55	NMX643	Leyland Leopard PSU3F/5R	Plaxton Supreme IV	C53F	1980	0887	1087	Ex Mayne (HDB355V)
2	SCP342L	Leyland Leopard PSU4B/2R	Plaxton Derwent	B45F	1973	1087	0188	Ex WYT(3002) via Mayne.
55	GRF267V	Leyland Leopard PSU3E/4R	Duple Dominant II Express	C53F	1980	1287	1088	Returned to Mayne again.
	VUB400H	Leyland Leopard PSU3A/4R	Plaxton Panorama Elite	C53F	1970	1287	0288	For spares only.

1988

Acquired with the business of Lymmville Coaches, Lymm, Cheshire:

f/no.	Reg/n	Chassis Details	Bodywork Details	Seating Capacity	New	In	Out	Notes
	PLG503L	Bedford YRQ	Duple Dominant	C45F	1973	0188	0388	
	PLG367P	Bedford YRQ	Duple Dominant	C45F	1976	0188	0190	Traded in by Mayne
	FCW808S	Bedford YMT	Duple Dominant II	C53F	1978	0188	0190	Traded in by Mayne
	CAL584T	Bedford YMT	Duple Dominant II	C53F	1979	0188	0388	
	FEK187V	Bedford YLQ	Duple Dominant II	C53F	1980	0188	0489	
	EHB259G	Leyland Leopard PSU4A/2R	East Lancashire	B43F	1969	0288	00	Ex Stonier, Goldenhill
	ODM500V	Leyland Leopard PSU3E/4R	Duple Dominant II Express	C49F	1979	0388	0690	Ex Crosville
6	UJX916M	Leyland Leopard PSU4B/2R	Plaxton Derwent	B45F	1973	0488	00	Ex Mayne.

1989

f/no.	Reg/n	Chassis Details	Bodywork Details	Seating Capacity	New	In	Out	Notes
27	F27HNC	DAF SB2305DHTD585	Duple 320	C57F	1989	0189		Became 614BWU in 1190
7	JWU252V	Leyland Leopard PSU4C/4R	Plaxton Derwent	B43F	1975	0189	0490	Ex Mayne.
	MWW563P	Leyland Leopard PSU3C/4R	Plaxton Supreme Express	C49F	1976	0289	1091	Ex West Yorkshire (2547). Became UCE665 1090, then RMA734P in 1091
55	GRF267V	Leyland Leopard PSU3E/4R	Duple Dominant II Express	C53F	1980	0389	0190	Ex Mayne.
12	RKH312T	Leyland Leopard PSU3E/4R	Plaxton Supreme IV	C49F	1979	0489	1093	Ex Scarborough & District (195) as 165DKH. Was originally FAG195T.

f/no.	Reg/n	Chassis Details	Bodywork Details	Seating Capacity	New	In	Out	Notes
1990								
	C520WBF	Leyland Tiger TRCTL11/3RZ	Duple 340	C50Ft	1986	0290	0994	Ex Mayne. Became FIL9386 in 0290.
	OVC958P	Leyland Leopard PSU3C/4R	Plaxton Supreme Express	C49F	1976	0590	1091	Ex Midland Red South (68). Was JOX454P, then 491GAC.
51	A351KBA	Bedford PJK	Plaxton Supreme IV	C29F	1984	1190	0393	Ex Mayne. Became CSU918 in 0991. Traded in by Mayne.
1991								
28	H28FVM	Dennis Javelin 11SDL1921	Duple 320	C55F	1991	0591		
	NHL201R	Leyland Leopard PSU5A/4R	Duple Dominant	C57F	1977	0891	1194	Became DIL6907 by 0992
29	J29LJA	Dennis Javelin 11SDL1921	Duple 320	C55F	1991	0891		
	LIW1324	Leyland Leopard PSU3C/2R	Willowbrook	B51F	1976	0291	0092	Ex Mayne (NTX361R).
	NTX363R	Leyland Leopard PSU3C/2R	Willowbrook	B51F	1976	0391	0092	Ex Mayne.
61	NIB3261	Leyland Leopard PSU5C/4R	Plaxton Supreme IV	C57F	1981	1291		Ex Mayne (SNC361X).
1994								
10	KUC969P	Leyland Fleetline FE30ALR	Metro Cammell Weymann	H45/32F	1976	0194	0394	On loan from Mayne.
1	OJD131R	Leyland Fleetline FE30AGR	Park Royal	H44/29F	1976	0194	0394	On loan from Mayne.
	WPD28Y	Leyland Leopard PSU3G/4R	ECW	C49F	1982	0394	1194	
1	OJD131R	Leyland Fleetline FE30AGR	Park Royal	H44/29F	1976	0594		Ex Mayne.
4	GND505N	Daimler Fleetline CRG6LXB	Northern Counties	H43/32F	1974	0794		Ex Mayne.
10	KUC969P	Leyland Fleetline FE30ALR	Metro Cammell Weymann	H45/32F	1976	0794		Ex Mayne.
	ARB134T	Leyland Leopard PSU3E/4R	Plaxton Supreme Express	C49F	1979	0994		Ex Trent via Mayne.
	BRC140T	Leyland Leopard PSU3E/4R	Plaxton Supreme Express	C49F	1979	0994	1094	Ex Trent via Mayne.
3	YNA328M	Daimler Fleetline CRG6LXB	Northern Counties	H43/32F	1973	0994		
	SCH149X	Leyland Leopard PSU3F/4R	Willowbrook 003	C49F	1982	0994		Ex Trent via Mayne (had been stored).
	PCW680P	Leyland Leopard PSU3C/4R	Duple Dominant Express	C53F	1976	1294		
1995								
	KVO142W	Leyland Leopard PSU3E/4R	Willowbrook 003	C49F	1980	0195		Ex Trent via Mayne (stored since 0894).

PHOTOCREDITS

The principal photographer in this volume is Brian Lomas, except as shown below.

AEC	14 (top), 16 (bottom)
D. Barrow	71 (bottom), 76 (lower)
A. Byrom	27 (bottom right)
D. Foster	46 (bottom), 92 (centre)
A. Greaves	49 (bottom)
C. W. Heaps	24 (lower left & right)
A. Ingram	12 (bottom)
M. King	34 (bottom)
G. Lumb	Rear cover
R. F. Mack	25 (centre left), 30 (top), 31 (top)
R. Marshall	19 (bottom), 20 (centre), 21 (bottom), 22 (bottom), 25 (top left), 29 (top)
A. Mayne & Son Ltd	6 (bottom), 7, 8, 9 (all), 10 (top), 11 (both), 28 (bottom), 35 (top left), 36 (top), 43 (top left & right), 48 (bottom), 70 (bottom)
E. Ogden Collection	22 (centre), 23 (top & centre), 31 (centre & bottom), 32 (bottom), 33 (centre), 43 (bottom left & right), 44 (top & bottom), 45 (lower), 48 (top)
Park Royal Coachbuilders	15 (both)
H. W. Peers	26 (top)
H. S. Postlethwaite	39 (bottom), 40 (top), 44 (centre)
B. A. Ridge	30 (bottom)
J. Senior	Front cover, 84 (top), 92 (lower both), 93 (both), 96
Senior Transport Archive	16 (top), 74 (lower), 75 (upper), 79 (lower)
G. H. Smith	24 (upper right)
Unknown	20 (bottom), 22 (top), 23 (bottom), 24 (upper left), 25 (upper left, plus centre left & right), 26 (centre), 27 (bottom left), 30 (centre), 32 (top)

The signwriting and livery say it all as Scania M211 NDB heads towards the Arndale Bus Station from Piccadilly Bus Station before the remodelling of the latter began on Monday, 18th September 1995.